C000116776

What a World

Compiler and Editor

Geoffrey Duncan

Textile Art

Pamela Pavitt

ISBN 0 85346 212 7
© The United Reformed Church, 2002

Compiled and Edited by Geoffrey Duncan
Textile Art by Pamela Pavitt

Published by Granary Press
the imprint of The United Reformed Church
86 Tavistock Place, London WC1H 9RT

Produced by Communications and Editorial, Graphics Office

Printed by Healeys Printers, Unit 10, The Sterling Complex,
Farthing Road, Ipswich, Suffolk IP1 5AP

Contents

We are extremely grateful

to Carol Rogers for her faith and enthusiasm since the very first conversation about the anthology;

to Sara Foyle who worked with unflagging energy in designing the cover and format of the book as she juggled with pictures and text;

to Katia Muscará who used her expertise in photographing the textile art.

This has been a time consuming piece of work for the staff and we are pleased to have experienced the patience and endurance of the United Reformed Church Communications and Editorial, Graphics Office.

Many, many thanks.

Geoffrey Duncan and Pamela Pavitt

Foreword

**"A generation goes, and a generation comes,
but the earth remains forever."**

(Eccles 1.4)

Eternal though many of the Preacher's verities might be, he inhabits
a different world. Literally. Generations before ours may have lived
in constant fear that the earth would *not* remain forever, but ours is
the first with the ability *ourselves* to ensure that it might not. The threat that we shall end it
all in one evil puff may be slightly less real than it was, but our assault on our planet's resources,
beauty, harmony and equilibrium continues apace. At some point, and who knows how soon,
a generation might go and another not come, and the earth might not have remained forever.
And whom shall we blame but ourselves.

Things wouldn't be quite so bad if we weren't in denial about it, if we lived as though we
did take seriously the present and future consequences of our actions. But we do not even
confront the problem, let alone consider how we might change our behaviour to give our
planet a chance. Our politicians, our media, our opinion formers – few are prepared to make
plain the reality, to jolt us into confronting how our behaviour in the north impacts adversely
on our sisters and brothers in the south and our shared – and only – source of life. If we would
'only connect'…

With its powerful words and striking art this book will help us to make those connections and
inspire us to keep the state of our world before us. It is a unique resource in terms both of
concept and content, and no one using it will feel other than deep gratitude to Pamela and to
Geoff for their vision, inspiration, and sheer hard work in compiling and creating it. It is an
abundance of riches which will serve us well in our worship, in our private devotions and in
many other contexts. But while informing, inspiring and challenging us, it will also lead us to
action. Even a casual dip into its pages will leave us sitting uncomfortably in our armchairs or
pews, concerned to turn prayer into practice, reflection into response, understanding into
undertaking. Anything less would be profoundly to misunderstand the intent of the compilers.

As people who take seriously our Lord's prayer that the reign of God come and the will of
God be done on earth as it is in heaven, we cannot stand by while the very opposite happens.
The scriptures nowhere suggest that a hope of heaven exonerates us from a concern – indeed,
a passion – to protect our environment, see that justice prevails, and make real our Lord's deep
longing that all should have life and have it in abundance. If this beautiful volume helps inspire
and resource us for the struggle, its editors will not have laboured in vain. And the words of
Qohelet might not sound quite so complacent…

Andrew Bradstock
Secretary for Church and Society
United Reformed Church

Creation Care

Creating God, you have given us a vision of a new heaven and a new earth ...
resources conserved
earth tended
atmosphere cleansed
trees planted
injustice ended
oceans teeming
nations at peace

Creator, Redeemer, Sustainer,
alert nations, enthuse churches,
receive our commitment and so entwine our lives with Your purpose.
earth and heaven will then sing of your glory.

Amen

Environmental Issues Network
Churches Together in Britain and Ireland

The above prayer is commended by church leaders from Britain and Ireland for use prior to, during, and after the Earth Summit 2002.

Introduction

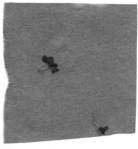

Many people live in communities where they are able to give praise and thanksgiving for the beauty of creation; for the loveliness of land and sea; for air that is fresh and can be breathed happily; for gentle, flowing streams and rivers. There is the majestic grandeur of snow-peaked mountains, the exhilaration of surf-boarders as they attach themselves to the flowing waves with golden sands awaiting their arrival; the excitement of the downhill ski run; the gentle walk among the rolling hills which provide a part of life for many fortunate people whether through daily living or when on holiday.

Many people live on battered, graffitti ridden, housing estates; experience the restricting atmosphere of inner city living; make an exciting visit with inner city school children to a city farm; suffer stress from faceless management structures; live with the pain of unemployment and job-searching or try to rise from the stigma of homelessness.   In some countries land is arid, rock or sand strewn; air is polluted by emissions of toxic materials; rivers have dried up because the rains have failed; there are hot, humid conditions where monsoon and tidal waves destroy lives, livelihood and property; the ecology of the land denies the opportunity to grow basic food for families with some left over to sell at the local market as a source for income generation; there is no clean water for more than a billion people; some people have to buy their water from multi-national corporations whilst there is plenty of free water for swimming pools; there are people who are physically and mentally impaired – and their numbers are vast – in every part of our global community. Indigenous people in Botswana, Australia, Aotearoa New Zealand, the amazing Amazonian jungles and the interior parts of Karnataka State, south India, all have a right to live by their own cultures and not to fear the power of the multi-national corporations which slash the rain forests, ruin their lands and work with stealth to take over crops and staple food farming for profit and power. Innocent people live continually in fear because of war and civil strife. There is the destroyed country of Afghanistan; bullet-littered Israel/Palestine and the continuing threat of international terrorism. All of these are places and situations where ecology and the environment impact upon daily lives.

Our local environment is precious. It needs to be developed and maintained but if we remain only there – in that small area of God's creation – our own backyard, we shall discover it is too small for life today therefore, we must consider the global situation. The now well-worn phrase comes to mind – 'act locally but think globally'.

Some time ago I spoke with Pamela Pavitt about compiling an anthology in which Pamela's wonderful textile art would be related with the theme. During discussion we realised that an anthology based on ecology, environment and justice would be an interesting project. These three major concerns impact upon global communities in different and varied ways. Some aspects but by no means all have been included in this book. We hope that people will be motivated to use the material in public worship, personal meditation and thought, silence and retreats, including ecumenical and inter-faith activities. Also, we believe it will be beneficial if programmes are initiated in secular society such as building a relationship with the supermarket chains and local shopping malls. It is timely to reflect upon progress that has been made since the first Earth Summit – United Nations Conference on Environment and Development – in Rio 1992. Now, it is time to consider how more support and activity can be encouraged to keep alive the important decisions requiring action which will be necessary after the Earth Summit in Johannesburg 2002.

As communities learn to acknowledge and love each other there may be more opportunity to love global creation and global life.

Geoffrey Duncan
April 2002

Communion and Creation

Bread is broken, wine is poured; here before us is the Lord. In Holy Communion, the gifts of creation are joined with the sufferings of Christ to offer new life.

Week in, week out, across the nations, in many different languages, Christian people gather together to share in a meal that is both simple and profound. It is simple in that it is about eating bread and drinking wine. It is profound, in that the eternal mystery of God's love in Jesus Christ is once again made present.

At the heart of the Christian faith lies the table of the Lord, the place of offering of the broken bread, sign of the offering of the broken body. The fruit of the earth, that of grain and of the vine are taken. In them are seen the suffering body and blood of Christ. Through them is the risen life of Christ made known.

The people of God gather around the Lord's table to share in communion with the Lord and with one another. This communion unites the saints across the ages and across the nations in one body.

In the mystery of this offering, God's work of redemption and creation are drawn together. Here are no fancy words or long speeches. Physical things are taken to become food for life in all its fullness. In this act of communion creation is redeemed and given hope. Through the act of creation, communion becomes possible. Creation and communion are interwoven at the heart of the life of faith.

Bread and wine speak both of death and of Resurrection.

In remembering the suffering and death of Jesus, so we remember those suffering and dying across the world. In remembering the resurrection of Jesus, so we claim the promise of new life for wounded peoples and a wounded world.

The concern for the whole of God's world lies at the heart of the Christian faith. This is not just in the words of pious preachers who urge the people to ever new efforts of care. This is not just in the small acts of charity by which we seek to salve our consciences. This concern is about sharing in God's loving action in the world, already laid bare in the offering of Jesus Christ.

Gathering at the Lord's table and receiving the bread and the wine both unites us with God and creation and renews us for participating in God's work in the world. God has already opened the way to the transformation of the world in the death and resurrection of Jesus Christ. Our work is to share in that transformation, in our own lives and amongst the people and places who cry out daily in need.

Elizabeth Welch
England

With love to our families and friends – along with the women and men who use their skills - and the people as yet unknown to us, who benefit from K'halli (page 40)

Geoffrey Duncan and Pamela Pavitt

A Cameo of Creation

For the Beauty of All Creation

Lord of all life,
thank you for the beauty of trees and flowers,
minerals and earth,
animals and birds.
Help me to become a wise steward of your creation and
a good tenant of your world;
so that, together with my neighbours in Christ
– present and future –
I will see nature as your gift
that I should plunder less and replenish more.

Amen

Kevin Fray
England

A Litany of Air, Sea and Earth

God of eagles
you know where we are going
and what we must do
to fulfil our potential.
Fly above us
shelter us under your wings.

All: **God of all creatures of the air, fly above us.**

Christ of dolphins
when we play in the shallows
or flounder in deep water
you have already been there.
Swim alongside us
sharing our joys and entering our pain.

All: **Christ of all creatures of the sea, swim alongside us.**

Spirit of moles
sent to empower us,
to delve into tunnels
linking our selves to each other.
Burrow within us
making our lives your home.

All: Spirit of all creatures of the earth, burrow within us.

Trinity of all living things
of air, sea and earth,
we feel your presence
and worship your creativity.

All: Trinity of air, sea and earth, we worship your creativity.

Heather Johnston
England

Creation Thoughts

Sea

Rolling and crashing: moving or calm,
Bearer of trade-ships from near and far,
Element of fishes, adored by yachtsmen.

Earth

Shaped by the wind and the rain and the ice,
Moulded by farmers, adapted by quarrymen,
Changed by sawyers and cut by roadmen.

Air

Over the land and the wide open oceans,
Tempest and whirlwind and soft gentle breezes,
Medium for aircraft and birds in their flight.

Pamela Pavitt
England

A Song of Love

Love makes Creation one,
a universe of care,
the love that gave all space and time for all life to share
that all as branches of one tree
may live a life that's full and fair.

Love was made plain in Christ,
a human life on earth,
a love that gave and died to bring a new life to birth,
to sow the strength and power of love
and teach us our eternal worth.

Love lives among us here,
the Spirit's gift of grace,
uniting all that lives in one great loving embrace,
to build a world that's just and free,
a world that has for all a place.

Tune: Love Unknown

William Whitson
England

A Song for All God's Creatures

A rainbow in the sky
recalls God's faithful word:
the promise that he makes to us
and every beast and bird.

To all he gives this earth,
to tigers, snakes and dogs,
to blackbirds, dolphins, elephants,
to horses, cats and frogs.

The sheep that clothe the hills,
the cattle in the fields,
they, too, are here to share with us
the goodness God's earth yields.

And so give thanks to God
for life and joy and friends,
for love that every life can share -
a love that never ends.

Tune: Sandys

William Whitson
England

What a World

Children's Song

Adam in his garden
gave each beast a name:
with our fav'rite animals
we do the same.

Rusty the retriever,
Marigold the mouse;
Borodin the budgie
trilling through the house.

Jezebel the gerbil,
Roderick the rat;
Romeo the rabbit,
Catherine the cat.

Gloria the goldfish,
Hollyhock the horse;
Gabriel the guinea-pig
(well-bred, of course).

Hannibal the hamster,
Samuel the snake;
Deirdre the delightful duck
and Dan the drake.

For these charming creatures
we are asked to care;
all the world's a garden,
God has put us there.

Tune: Glenfinlas

David Mowbray
England

One Flower

Hard!
       Harsh!
              Dry!
                     Drab!

A single flower
Can contradict!

David J Harding
England

Rural and Real

Landscape of loveliness
greened brown and
cultivated,
strangely wild
with gentle harshnesses
of interwoven
promises and threats:

the sky-embracing trees
and ground-hugging grass,
field, hedge and lane,
patch-worked and various,
meeting the needs
of life and death,
growth and decay:

food for the table
and the foxes' lair,
the dining-rooms
of sheep and hawks and worms,
of birds that sing,
hedgehogs and fleas;

bright ante-rooms
of abattoirs,
sun-traps for warmth
and sheltered spots
and space to walk
and much to paint
and all to reproduce
and represent ...

movement and stillness
now
between each then and then ...

a worthwhile gift
of awesome usefulness.

David J Harding
England

Summer Pasture

Among these green encircling hills
deciding to be mountains at the valley's end
time tocks irrelevantly.

Mr Davis's cows flow
regular as tides
between the milking shed and meadow,
but apart from that,
and the sun's broad rhythm
tipping the see-saw shadows
over the hill at cockcrow
and back again for twilight,
who can tell the soft creeping of days?

For a while Nellie forgets her pups
to round up seven sheep;
somewhere it must be market day
out there beyond the forest.

Shall we amble to the village for a paper
learn what the world fights over for today
or let it wait another week without us?

Cecily Taylor
England

We Gaze in Wonder at the Morning's Dawning

We gaze in wonder at the morning's dawning,
Positive witness to God's faithful grace;
We turn our backs, and in the shadow standing,
Shield the light we need to find our place.

In arrogance, in darkness we will stumble,
Until we turn to face that dawning light.
We venerate our skill, the rocket's rumble,
Deadens sense, distorting wrong and right.

As stewards of love, let's contemplate creation,
filigree frosting of a winter's pain;
God holds in hand elation, desperation,
Born in death that we might gain.

Andrew Pratt
England

Visitor

I glance through my window
desk top forgotten.
On the hanging nuts
a majestic bird –
red skull cap and pants
black and white cloak;
the spotted woodpecker's
determined tree-chipping beak
finds another occupation.

You have no greater admirer
little friend
honouring our garden
with your presence.

Now you are gone
what is left
but to return to the keyboard
use other trees
echo your tap-tap-tap?

Cecily Taylor
England

The Dawn-Light

Still in the dawn-light
of our budding day
shyly we reach out,
awed to touch yet bound to grasp
our lovely love
rich beauty
dazzling to our earliest glimpse
yet ever since
becoming brighter every way,
splendoured with promises
that who dare say
we are awake enough to see
more than a dream
of all that is to be?

David J Harding
England

Solomon's Glory

Azaleas in the spring clothed with colour,
tall chestnuts with glowing candles,
laburnums and wattles dripping gold,
the pansies, wallflowers and violets,
the pink and blue hydrangeas,
and the lilies exotic and pungent
or white as snow –

Why, what can Solomon in all his glory
          show like one of these?

          For all delight
          in flora's dress,
          for daily sight
          of happiness,
          we pray a Grace –
          we've glimpsed your face.

Bernard Thorogood
Australia

Thank You for Plants

Thank You, God:
for the plants which live in so many varied
climates
around the world;
for flowers with their shapes,
fragrances and colours
which give us pleasure in gardens;
for plants that provide our food,
eaten at many different mealtimes;
for wood and timber that is grown and
forested
to provide furniture for our homes;
for special plants which have healing properties
in their leaves and roots
which can cure illnesses
Thank You, Creator God.
Amen

Pamela Pavitt
England

The Parable of the Bougainvillea

Consider the bougainvillea,
it grows, throwing a riot of flaming colour
across the dry, dusty, barren landscape.
When all seems dead and brown,
it grows,
not just alive,
but vivid, vibrant, shouting aloud.
And the drought cannot overcome it.
A message for us in this, perhaps,
when our world seems grey and drear,
insane, caught up in a tangled web of lies and intrigue,
hatred and disappointments.
Then, even then, there is life,
the spark of Christ within us,
not just alive,
but shouting, bursting out
with joy and singing,
to overcome,
to celebrate.

Jenny Spouge
England

A Hug for the Trees

I love to hug trees
today I gazed upon a magnificent nut tree
with its long shaggy bark
I went over to touch it
I even thought for a moment
I want a piece of her garment
I couldn't bring myself to injure her in any way
how difficult it is to hug her with all the
sharp stiff bark curling up.

I remembered my discomfort when
lots of people hugged me
now I hug people
now I hug trees

see Jane run
see Dick run
see what Godde can do!

Eleanore Milardo
USA

A Thought of Trees

Trees laugh at us,
laugh at our fussing fretting
having getting –
standing there for centuries
being
just being themselves.

They won't worry if their leaves
have failed to grow a hair's breadth
by next Tuesday week
or whether they'll produce
enough rich loam
to nourish them
and see them through another year.

Somewhere within their roots
they've grasped eternity.

I like to think near trees –
they sort me out;
I like to laugh with trees –
smile at my own fussing fretting
having getting;
I have to grow near trees –
concrete kills me.

Cecily Taylor
England

A Cameo of Nature

Here let's create a cameo of nature:
bluebell and sorrel from the woodland dell,
cornflower and poppy from the harvest acre,
tough heather from the moorland and the fell.
From meadows there'll be celandine and clover,
all in a space minute as convent cell.
Bright birds will quench their thirst by sparkling water
on land reclaimed for heaven from urban hell!

Grace Westerduin
England

Partners in Creation

Voice 1:   Almighty God,
             Creator of all living things in our world
             those that walk,
             that fly and glide,
             those that creep and burrow,
             that swim and dive,
             those that grow and flower.

All: **Teach us to enjoy our surroundings
             to preserve and not destroy any part of creation.
             Help us to respect and protect
             everything that lives in our world.**

Voice 2:   Lord Jesus,
             Saviour of all people
             the starving and thirsty, and the replete,
             the sick and dying, and the healthy,
             the homeless, and those who live in mansions,
             the neglected and abused, and the cherished
             the lonely, and those surrounded by people.

All: **Teach us awareness and understanding
             of all kinds of need.
             Help us to show love and care
             for everyone in our world.**

Voice 3:   Holy Spirit,
             actively working in our lives
             showing us truth and light,
             bringing freedom and peace
             giving us gifts of creativity,
             knowledge and technical skills,
             strength and leadership.

All: **Teach us to recognize
             and develop our skills and gifts.
             Help us to use them wisely
             for the continuing creation of our world.
             Amen**

Heather Johnston
England

A Song of the Seasons

Round the year the seasons follow, giving shape to life on earth.
Circling round and ringing changes, light and darkness, death and birth.
With delight we feel the magic, join our planet's joyful rhythm:
Frost and snowfall, rain and sunshine, setting for our fears and mirth.

Spring takes root in depths of winter, lifts the heart when buds appear.
Summer follows, warmth and sunshine, days of ease to crown the year.
Harvest home our labour blesses, leading on to autumn glory;
Winter evenings by the fireside, earth at rest, yet spring is near.

In the town we may not notice – turn the lights on, raise the heat;
Snow or sunshine, makes no difference, Nature's conquest is complete.
Street lights hide the night sky's beauty, who knows when the new moon's coming?
Waves may rise and winds may threaten – roads are safe beneath our feet.

Where's the joy and where's the wonder if our days are all the same?
We can dance to Nature's music if the seasons we reclaim.
Touch and taste and see and listen; eyes and ears and tongue and fingers
Find the soul in all creation, life's variety proclaim.

Tune: Scarlet Ribbons

William Whitson
England

A Prayer of Thanksgiving

Most Holy Trinity
we thank you for the beauty of your creation
and for the joy of living in a world so full of wonder,
may all nature join us in praise and worship
adoration and longing love, in response
to the gift of life you have given us.

Lord of all creation
may the beauty of this earth
lead us to a deeper worship of you.
A reverence that causes gentleness.
Fear that leads to holiness
and a peace we long to share.

Pat Randall
England

A Meditation

I told God that I found the world too hard to understand and too complicated to cure.

God nodded.
And then he took me to the fields around a town and asked me, as we walked, if there
wasn't something here that could inspire me.
I pointed out that I lived in the city and fields were too far from home.

God nodded.
And then he took me to the city streets and asked me, as we looked over a gate, if
there wasn't something in the garden to give me joy.
I reminded him that my home was on floor 7 where the view was grey, not green.

God nodded.
And then he took me to a block of flats and asked me, as we stared upwards at the
balconies, if the window boxes splashed with colour might not tell me something.
I muttered something about the luxury of flats with balconies.

God nodded.
And then he took me home to my cluttered lounge and asked me, as we put the vase
of poppies on the table, if there wasn't something glorious about the creation we held?

I nodded.

Neil Thorogood
England

Blessing for the Earth

That we, and all fellow creatures entrusted to our care, may praise you, we ask your blessing, heavenly Father.

Bless our house plants and window boxes, our bird feeders and our animal companions. For some of us it is especially through these that we praise you.

Bless those of us who, through your Son, in the power of your living Spirit, serve you and our fellow human creatures in cities.

Bless our rivers and rain, the butts in which we harvest the rain. Bless our compost which returns to the soil and rises again to new life as a symbol of resurrection.

Bless our parks and gardens, the living soil communities with which we praise you and within which we too are organisms. The flowers praise you in their radiance, our vegetables and fruit praise you in their beauty. Through nurturing them we enable your will to be done on earth as it is in heaven. We contribute to biodiversity and to right relationships among all creatures.

Bless our efforts to share earth's beauty, its fruits and life. These are yours, which you share with us, and entrust to our subordinate rule, that we too may share with your other creatures. For you love all that you have created. Through your Son, Jesus Christ our Lord, you have reconciled ourselves and all the earth's creatures which you created.

Bless us as we offer the praise of all creation to you, through your Son, in the Holy Spirit.

Edward P Echlin
England

Coconut Tree

My tired eyes
seek rest
in your leaves
majestic assembly of hundreds
dainty green fingers
each dances graciously
in tune of ocean breeze
whose lutes play
millions melodies various
from subdued silence
to untempered out cry

Your stage
is the lofty blue
eternal throne of god
the infinite inspiration innumerable
blessed by sun god
the source of all life
as free gifts it imparts
on all earth
golden ray abundant
of its own being

To give life
to every living thing
Human species
Animal species
Plants and fish
Never asking
who's more precious
whose principle is
equality, freedom and love
directing to the true peace
which was in the beginning
and shall come at last

Some call it shalom
Some call it grace or kingdom
Others name it otherwise

My stifling mind
gazes on your trunk
standing tall and gracious
bending and unbending
caressed and battered

by wind, people, other creatures
Yet never accepting
to be broken down
nor torn apart
within yourself
on your own accord

May your own strength
be my own
May your wisdom
be my own

My broken heart
yearns for your fruits
The cosy clusters
round and solid
growing on the tree top
sweet and cool water
the inward spring spontaneous
shielded by self protective hardshell
to quench thirst
of people in toil
to survive under tropical heat
And your meat to nourish
the poor of south

Your shells are used
for creative images of art work
or to be offered for fuel

Your message is
to say 'No' to any waste
and 'Halt' to all wastefulness
of greed and domination

Oh, coconut tree
of the south
a being that is heart warming
a presence revealing a truth
of God Universal
The eternal source of all life

Sun-Ai Lee Park
Malaysia

A Prayer of Intercession

Father of all,
Creator beyond time,
    we think of the flow of seasons and generations that is our home.

We remember those who have lived before us:
those whose explorations have left us gifts of knowledge and expertise,
those whose hard work has been the foundation for our prosperity,
those whose sacrifices have become the stuff of our legends,
those whose faithfulness has challenged our ambivalence.

We dream of those who will live long after we are gone:
the great, great grandchildren who will know us as ancient pictures,
the generations of every nation who will trace history back to us,
the people who will shape the world, in part, upon the lessons we demonstrated,
the believers who will know you, a little, through our testimony.

Past and future meet in our presence.
So we pray for ourselves and those of our generation:
that we will hand on a world worthy of humanity and of you, eternal God,
that we will measure our treatment of creation against the needs of those unborn,
that we will treasure our world and protect it from ourselves,
that we will be so inspired by your Spirit that our work will bear distant fruit.

And to you, eternal and intimate God,
    be all glory, praise and honour,
    as it was in the beginning,
    is now,
    and for ever shall be,
    world without end.
Amen.

Neil Thorogood
England

A Prayer of Praise

Praise be to God for nesting boxes,
    crocus bulbs and butterflies,
        for tadpole ponds and window boxes and trellises by the door.
Praise be to God for grass that's cut and grass gone wild,
    for trees that tower,
        leaves being raked,
           and soil to be dug.
Praise be to God for seedlings and cuttings,
    hedges and patios,
        bushes in bud and hedgehogs.
Praise be to God for a world on our doorsteps!
Amen.

Neil Thorogood
England

A Song for Our Town

Here are the homes and the streets where we live,
here are the people we meet every day:
parents and children and neighbours and friends,
sharing the place where we sleep, work and play.

Churches and offices, factories and schools,
houses and gardens and trees growing tall,
places for shopping and parks to enjoy –
this is our town and a home for us all.

This is our holy land, built for our dreams;
Christ walks among us here, making us free;
filled with the Spirit and sharing God's love
we can make our town a good place to be.

Tune: Bonnie George Campbell

William Whitson
England

Poppies

From a Welsh friend came native poppies –
yellow flowers and a few shoots –
brought to keep memories green and give them roots.

A bare patch in the garden they filled –
or would when fully grown.
Once planted, they were left alone.

Next year, they grew and flourished
bringing yellow sunshine to that space
and smiling memories of a friendly face.

In two years yellow flowers appeared garden-wide.
Wind-blown and bird-scattered,
Welsh wizardry grinned at us from every side.

Soon neighbours' gardens, boundary walls
and cracked paving stones had their share.
Green shoots and budding heads and yellow flowers –
our friend is everywhere.

Unchecked, those seeds by friendship sown will spread,
Look at the flowers and learn – as Jesus said.

Marjorie Dobson
England

The Desert Bloomed

There had been an amazing change in the weather. After a build-up of heat over a few weeks there were occasional thunder showers preceded by branch-snapping winds and a collection of profuse grey clouds created a humid atmosphere.

Heavy rains came. There were two days of almost continuous rain which fell across the east of the country and in much of South Africa. After the rains the dry, dusty bushland behind our house had been transformed into a water world. On approaching a newly created lake we could hear the loud chirpings of frogs and many of them were hopping around. The next day there were no frogs but a lot of frogspawn and the day after there were many tadpoles swimming freely. A few days later we were perplexed to see what looked like, from a distance, masses of white paper floating on the water. However, on getting closer, we found lilies, white and pink, which had appeared as if from nowhere on the pond, stretching into the clearings between thorn trees as far as we could see. The lilies bloomed exquisitely. The tadpoles got larger.
How long was it since conditions were right in this dry veld for lilies to bloom and frogs to spawn. There are times when wonder at God's creation takes one's breath away.

Brian Savage
Botswana/Tanzania

A Litany of Celebration for Our Creation

In the beginning God created the heavens and the earth.
God said: 'Let there be light,'
and day and night began:

We praise you, creating God,
for the gentle turn of day and night with their rhythm of work and rest.

God said: 'Let there be room above the waters,'
and the sky appeared:

We praise you, creating God,
for the beauty and majesty of the blue sky with its clouds and many moods.

God said: 'Let the water hold together in one place,'
and dry land emerged from sea:

We praise you, creating God,
for the stunning power of the oceans and the breath-taking beauty of landscape.

God said: 'Let things grow everywhere,'
and from the tiniest moss to the mightiest tree the plants emerged:

We praise you, creating God,
for the super-abundance of plants and the rich variety of resources they provide.

God said: 'Let there be lights in the sky,'
and suns, planets and moons began their orbits:

We praise you, creating God,
for the scale of the universe with all its secrets to inspire our awe.

God said: 'Let there be life,'
and fish began to swim as birds took to the air:

We praise you, creating God,
for the life that teems in waters and the glorious sight of birds on the wing.

God said: 'Let there be animals,'
and across the land ran, hopped and crawled a wonderful horde.

We praise you, creating God,
for all the creatures sharing our land and the ways they help and sustain us.

God said, 'Let there be people,'
and in God's own image came women and men.

We praise you, creating God,
for our gift of life in creation and your call to care for all that you have made.

Neil Thorogood
England

Song of The Charente *

Dawn seeps through –
Dew-dusted, shining …
Veining off the velveting
Brevity of night;
Natures rises,
Driven from her dreaming –
Streaming, teeming
Into the light.

Gnarled old toad
Bellows in the shallows,
Water boatmen scuttle –
And the surface holds …

River, bearing secrets,
Life-force, and coolness,
Ancient, ceaseless,
Ceaseless flows away –
And the old cock scratches
In the distant farmyard,
Shouting, shouting,
Shouting at the day.

Barley stands
And shimmers in the sunlight –
Hushed like the brush
Of a feather on the air;
Wild oats scattering,
Bending over feathering,
Rustling and whispering –
Growing where they dare …
And butterflies go dancing,
Dancing in the day-glow,
Fluttering and flirting –
Oblivious there.

Early hot sky,
Enamelled blue molten,
Hides in its light
The ebullient flow
Of the lark –
His one eye glancing
At the gates of Heaven,
And his other eye fixed
On the earth far below …

Where vines march, close-ranked,
Green-flanked, twining –
Leaning to the autumn,
And the promise to come …
Longing for the lusciousness,
Sweet-lipping, tongue-slipping,
Easy deliciousness
Of harvest home!

And sunflowers stand
Ingot-gold, smiling …
Their seed-heavy heads –
Since summer is begun –
Keep turning, turning,
Subtly, silently –
Following, following,
The course of the sun …

For the sun shines down,
Penetrating crevices –
Bleaching the old stones,
Baking the clay
Of the terra-cotta tiles
On the tumbling buildings –
Burnishing the fabric
Of the passing day;
And the old bell strikes
From the tomb-cool chapel –
Calling, calling
To work and to pray.

So the warm light holds
Long into the evening,
Till the soil sleeps, thirsty,
Waiting for the dew …
And the river keeps flowing,
Secret, knowing,
Sleepless in the darkness …
Till the dawn seeps through.

* Charente lies inland of the west coast of France.

Margot Arthurton
England

Creation and Destruction

Touched by this dawn
the clay-wrought birds
take wing and sing
warm in the sun.

The songbirds turn
through fear to stone
On the petrified bough
in the ultimate storm.

Grace Westerduin
England

Words A Waterfall

I watched a waterfall today
rushing down the rocks
moulded into steps
bubbling,
     foaming,
          teaming with excitement

it reached its deepest level
to form a quiet, still pool
then flowed on ahead

Godde's words a waterfall within
when I hear them
I'm bubbling, teeming with excitement
then quiet to absorb all that's said

when I am filled
to overflowing
I then can tell my
story of what Godde said.

Eleanore Milardo
USA

The River

It is cool in the shadows,
And the weed pulls slow
In the deep-dark current
Concealed below.

It is deep in the river,
And the fish slip slow –
Sculling in the stream-wake
Lazily below.

There are ripples on the surface –
Shimmering, aglow,
Reflecting from the secrets
Buried below.

There is age in the river –
Too old to know ...
Forever seeing life
As the waters flow ...

For water is life
Whereby all things grow,
And only the river
Shall its secrets know ...

Margot Arthurton
England

Beauty and Compassion

Creating God
For the beauty of the earth, we praise you

  silence

For the ugly of the earth, we confess our sorrow

  silence

For the leaders of the world, we pray for their compassion and care

  silence

For the healing of the earth we make our own commitments

  silence
Amen.

David Pickering
England

Mission and Witness

Creating God,
For the magnificence and beauty of the earth, we offer our praise.
For our poor stewardship of your gift, we bring our confession.
We seek Your forgiveness and Your way.

May leaders act with courage and conviction.
May Your Church be inspired in its mission and witness.
We pray that our commitments and actions may heal your creation.

David Pickering
England

A Collect

Almighty God, maker of heaven and earth,
For the magnificence and beauty of all that is, we praise you
For the scarring of your gift we offer our confession
For governments and leaders, we pray for wise council
For the healing of creation we bring our own commitments.

David Pickering
England

The World Belongs to God

The world belongs to God,
    the earth and all its people.
How good and how lovely it is
    to live together in unity.
Love and faith come together,
    justice and peace join hands.
If the Lord's disciples keep silent,
    these stones would shout aloud.
Lord, open our lips
    and our mouths shall proclaim your praise.

Source unknown

God Has Given

God has given us creation, deep blue oceans, rivers, seas,
Humankind in all its glory, green of grass and yellow fields,
God has given us in nature, golden sun and rich brown earth,
Ours the task to make a harvest of each individual birth.

God has given us each other, red the blood that we all share,
Red the wine we drink together when we show God that we care.
God has given us our neighbours, each as different as can be,
From the richness of each culture God composed his harmony.

God has given us a promise, rainbow colours in the sky,
When the storm is at its fiercest, we believe God hears our cry.
God has given us a Saviour, Christ is risen from the dead,
Life he brings to all his people, light eternal, broken bread.

Tune: Clementine

Colin Ferguson
England

You Placed Us On This Earth

Creator God,
You gave us the gift of life.
You placed us on this earth
          with its minerals and waters,
          flowers and fruits,
          living creatures of grace and beauty!
You gave us the care of the earth.

Source Unknown

Our Offering

Lord, amid our delight in and concern for the environment

We offer:

our minds to sense your purpose for creation;

our hearts to receive your calling;

our hands, to put visions and plans into action.

Amen

David Pickering
England

Bless the Lord

Bless the Lord all created things
Sing His praise and exalt Him, for ever.

Bless the Lord you sun and moon
Sing His praise and exalt Him, for ever.

Bless the Lord you towering mountains
Sing His praise and exalt Him, for ever.

Bless the Lord you mighty rivers,
Bless the Lord you raging waterfalls,
Sing His praise and exalt Him, for ever.

Bless the Lord you rain and snow
Bless the Lord as you water the earth
Sing His praise and exalt Him, for ever.

Bless the Lord you trees and flowers
Bless the Lord with your colour and beauty
Sing His praise and exalt Him, for ever.

Bless the Lord you dogs and cats
Sing His praise and exalt Him, for ever.

Bless the Lord you ducks that swim
Sing His praise and exalt Him, for ever.

Bless the Father, the Son and the Holy Spirit:
Sing His praise and exalt Him, for ever.

Jenny Spouge
England

What a World

Get Wise!

Creator Lord of Planet Earth

Creator Lord of planet earth,
this Eden is our home!
You bid us seek, from earliest days,
our neighbours; good, your highest praise,
the gift which is shalom.

Yet, Lord, with this your planet earth,
what is it we have done?
We envy others' lawful gain,
we murder wantonly like Cain,
and forfeit God's shalom.

Alas, this fragile planet earth
is not its Maker's dream!
We have polluted paradise,
cut forests down, let thistles rise
which threatens God's shalom.

With misplaced pride on planet earth
we build our towers to heaven
and burrows deep to test our strength,
unleashing power which will at length
adulterate shalom.

Creator Lord of planet earth,
Creator Spirit, come!
Help us to see this gem unpriced
more truly through they eyes of Christ
and celebrate shalom!

Tune: Repton

David Mowbray
England

Simplistic?

We go in our cars,
We do –
Well, we have to,
We'll be late
Otherwise …

It's only a little way,
Lots of stops and starts,
Lots of fumes.

It's hot,
The sun burns
Through the haze –
We can't see far,
Only a little way –
Lots of fumes.

We can't see the sky-hole
The sun burns through –
Because of the haze …
We do know it's stopped the rain
Somehow, though –
Not here, but in other places –

Stopped the rain
So nothing grows
Over there now …
Because we drive our cars here
And the rains stop there –
The crops fail –
So
When we drive here

We steal from their begging bowls.

Margot Arthurton
England

That Relentless Rush

Even as I pray, Lord,
I hear that relentless rush of motorway traffic,
that pounding of lorries, that accelerating shriek of motorbikes,
that distant whine of a jetplane.

Yesterday I was walking woodland paths nearby and
I could hear that same penetrating rumble,
masked by the leaves but buzzing still.
If I wake tonight in the small hours, that buzzing will be there.

I cannot change this, Lord, so maybe
it is I who must change:
change the noise that I add to the world's clamour;
change the background music that I often switch on,
to a more silent concentration
on the person I'm talking to
or on the work I'm doing;
change the focus of my attention to the sound of the birds,
the speech of my companions,
to the song of the angels.
Lord, all this will not happen when I snap my fingers.
But slowly, by your grace, slowly let it happen.

David Mowbray
England

Lord Have Mercy

Forgive, O Lord:
the greed that damages tomorrow's world to comfort today's;
the laziness that litters tomorrow's world to ease today's;
the lack of care that pollutes tomorrow's world to convenience today's;
the injustice that deprives tomorrow's world to enrich today's;
the stupidity that forgets tomorrow's world and lives for today's.
Lord have mercy,
Lord have mercy,
Lord have mercy.

Peter Graystone
England

Toxic Lifestyles

Toxic lifestyles, toxic waste
Toxic greed and toxic hate
Toxic dams and toxic dreams
Toxic water, toxic streams

Toxic power, toxic taste
Toxic rush and toxic haste
Toxic logging, toxic air
Toxic people, we don't care

Stop!

Listen to the voice of God
In the wilderness
In the emptiness

Still the storm of progress
Slow the avalanche of waste
Listen to the still small voice
Of calm.

Linda Jones
England

Greed

My heart chokes on the words
that leap out
'cyanide and dynamite used
to net a bigger catch of fish'.

My relative of the sea
treated with such horror
they are doing
it to me.

All life in the ocean
covered by many wounds.

Eleanore Milardo
USA

The Wise One

(based on Chief Seattle's reply and warning to 'The Great White Chief' in Washington 1854)

Group A: Listen to the Wise One,
            Hear his words of wisdom –
            Listen to him telling us
            That we are each a strand;
            With this web entrusted
            Into our safe keeping
            May we tend creation's wealth
            And reverence the land.

Group B: Listen to the oceans
            All the shining waters
            Sparkling from the springs of life –
            With all the welcome rains;
            Rivers are our brothers
            And deserve our kindness,
            Quenching thirst they treat us well –
            Their blood runs in our veins.

All: **We belong to the earth,**
            We belong to the mountains and plains;
            We are part of the web –
            And all the life it sustains.
            The world is ours if we share with all;
            Together we stand or fall,
            Stand or fall:
            Stand or fall.

Group A: Listen to the farmlands –
            Earth who is our mother
            Nourishes her children, we
            Exploit her bounteous year;
            Wisely used resources
            Honour the Creator –
            Safely guard the future days
            Of those who follow here.

Group B: Listen to the creatures –
            Whales and dolphins warn us,
            Buffalo and butterflies
            Are pleading as they fall;
            All in hedge and atoll
            Share our common birthright,
            Driven to extinction if
            The human plunders all.

All: We belong to the earth,
        We belong to the mountains and plains;
        We are part of the web –
        And all the life it sustains.
        The world is ours if we share with all;
        Together we stand or fall,
        Stand or fall:
        Stand or fall.

Group A: Listen to the wind's tale –
            Sweet the air of heaven,
            Perfumed by the meadow flowers
            All creatures breathe their share.
            Higher in the heavens
            We have been protected –
            Delicate the atmosphere
            To shield from heat and glare.

Group B: Listen to the woodlands
            Crying to the breezes –
            Halt the mighty jungle trees
            From thundering to their floor;
            Halt the creeping desert,
            Tend the field and forest –
            Earth without her leafy lungs
            Can nurture us no more.

All: We belong to the earth,
        We belong to the mountains and plains;
        We are part of the web –
        And all the life it sustains.
        The world is ours if we share with all;
        Together we stand or fall,
        Stand or fall:
        Stand or fall.

All: Listen to our children
        And their children's children
        Pleading for life's legacy –
        So what have we to give?
        Listen now and hurry –
        Use the fleeting minutes;
        If we heed the Wise One now
        Humanity could live.

All: We belong to the earth
        We belong to the earth –
        Together we stand or fall,

Solo Voice: Stand or fall –

All: Stand or fall.

Cecily Taylor
England

Pathway Through Recent Centuries

Creator God,
Thank you for the beauty and variety of our landscapes;
for green and pleasant lands.
Thank you for inspiring man to develop cog wheels and machinery.
Thank you for the discovery of coal, the power of steam, the making of steel
and the provision of electricity.
Thank you for the many inventions for industry and factories, for our homes
and transport.

But Oh! The carelessness for life, both human and animal;
for the devastation of much of the environment in which people live.
We spoil the green and pleasant lands;
We pollute the air with factory chimneys and car exhausts;
We use, often ruthlessly, the resources of the rich world;
We allow our cities to grow over the landscape;
We pollute our water and it becomes unclean.

Creator God,
Help us to plan wisely and give due value to all your creation.
Help us to understand more deeply, the relationship between people,
animals and plants.
Amen

Pamela Pavitt
England

Peace Process

From a compost heap
rises a tender shoot –
waste slowly turning
to fertile ground.

In a stark landscape
peace lifts a fragile shoot;
may all rains be gentle
no winds blow.

Cecily Taylor
England

From Garbage Dump to Healthy Living

We travelled by car to the Khaylasanahalli project on the edge of rural Bangalore from the centre of the fastest growing city in India, where traffic clogs the roads all day long and pollution is a way of life. Approaching K'halli, as it is popularly known, there are foul smelling garbage dumps which are operated by private companies on behalf of Bangalore city. At one time K'halli was a garbage dump but the State of Karnataka, which owned the four acre piece of land gave it to the Association for People with Disability, Bangalore for development as a Social and Therapeutic Horticultural Training Centre.

After the garbage had been removed the land was barren and undulating with gullies and boulders but there were fifty mango trees spread around the area. They were untended and in need of treatment. Skilled, knowledgeable people are now transforming this arid area into fertile and what will be water flow-controlled land, so that fruit trees, vegetables, cereal crops and medicinal plants can be grown as a part of the horticultural training scheme for physically and mentally impaired people. Also, there will be opportunities for income generation.

Already the mango trees have produced a crop of two hundred kilogrammes which was sold to local markets. Pumpkins are being grown and the crops will increase. A fine crop of maize was seen and future harvests will increase. A growing supply of medicinal plants will be tended and these are attracting interest from major pharmaceutical companies.

A former garbage dump is being transformed into a place where the continuing wonder of creation will enable more healthy living for humankind.

Geoffrey Duncan
England

Lord of the Wonder of Creation

Lord of the Wonder of Creation
      around the world,
we give thanks for the
different kinds of food that are grown
in diverse places,
      climates
            and conditions
for the betterment of humankind.

Lord of the Wonder of Creation
      around the world,
we give thanks for the
many different people
from diverse situations
      cultures
            and faith communities
who use their skills to benefit humankind.

Lord of the Wonder of Creation
      around the world,
we give thanks for
pumpkins and pomegranates
guavas and grapes
      coriander and cucumber
            red rice and raspberries
turnips and tomatoes.

Response: **Lord of the Wonder of Creation
around the world,
we pray that you will continue
to inspire and bless
the women and men
who are resourceful and resilient,
as they work the land.**

Geoffrey Duncan
England

Sidwell's Story

Sidwell, so the story goes, was a young Saxon woman from Exeter, south-west England, who used to take food to workers in the nearby fields but who was persecuted and killed by her stepmother. Where her blood fell, a new fountain sprung up on the site and later St Sidwell's Church, with its fresh water became known as a place of healing and wholeness.

Since 1997 an innovative and exciting project has been planned to convert the current St Sidwell's Church into a Community Centre, in the same tradition of refreshment and good health, with new facilities for local people. It has been designed to be multi-functional and to meet the needs of various community groups and individuals.

Together with nearby residents, organisations and businesses, the newly re-opened building seeks to make a difference to the area through a variety of activities – all with an emphasis on healthy living.

The Church has been converted to provide flats for local people, a community café with a training kitchen, an organic community garden, crèche and family workshops, a wide range of health activities and support groups, creative arts initiatives, a Lifelong Learning Centre, free IT workshops, re-cycling facilities with solar panels, complementary therapies, as well as a new Chapel and meeting rooms.

Over five hundred people from the local community have now become members of the St Sidwell's Centre. In one month alone over 5,000 different people came in to the re-formed 1950's church for one purpose or another.

In all, it is an excellent example of encouraging inclusive, sustainable living for the future and within the deep Judaeo-Christian tradition of offering hospitality and sustenance for human wellbeing.

If you find yourself in Exeter do call in for a drink and meet us!

Martyn Goss
England

Benedicite

Bless the Lord you can of lager
        (not upon the garden hedge);
Sing God's praise you chocolate wrapper
        (not upon the window ledge).
Bless the Lord you bold graffiti
        (not upon the bandstand);
Sing God's praise you sticky sweetie
        (not upon the grandstand).
Bless the Lord you paper tissue
        (not upon the park seat);
Sing God's praise you last Big Issue
        (not upon the side street).
Bless the Lord you fish and chip bag
        (not in market places);
Sing God's praise you salted crisp bag
        (not in open spaces).
O bless the Lord you litter bin
        and all the rubbish thrown within;
Gabriel, Raphael, Michael!
        archangels! help us to recycle.

David Mowbray
England

Stewards of Your World

The earth you give us for our needs
is not a place to waste and spoil,
we are but stewards of your world,
in trust – the seas, the air and soil;
so may we use with thought and care
your planet earth –
this is our prayer.

Cecily Taylor
England

Aboriginal Culture

Leader: In most aboriginal cultures of America, the earth is called 'Mother' as she is the source of blessings – food, clothing, shelter, medicines, beauty ... God, the Creator and source of life is called Great Spirit. Mother Earth speaks:

Voice: Listen, my children. The spirit who moved over the dry land is not pleased. I am thirsty. Are you listening?

All: **We are listening, Mother Earth. Speak.**

Voice: The spirit who filled the waters is not pleased. I choke with debris and pollution. Are you listening?

All: **We are listening, Mother Earth. Speak.**

Voice: The spirit who brought beauty to the earth is not pleased. I grow uglier everyday with misuse. Are you listening?

All: **We are listening, Mother Earth. Speak.**

Voice: The spirit who brought all the creatures of this earth is not pleased. My creatures are being destroyed. Are you listening?

All: **We are listening, Mother Earth. Speak.**

Voice: The spirit who gave humans life and a path to walk together is not pleased. You are losing your humanity and your footsteps stray from the path led by injustice. Are you listening?

All: **We are listening, Mother Earth.**
We are listening.

Leader: O God, you created the earth in goodness and in beauty. Forgive all that we have done to harm the earth.

All: **God, have mercy.**

Leader: O God, you have filled the earth with food for our sustenance.
Forgive us for not sharing the gifts of the earth.

All: **Christ, have mercy.**

Leader: You have created us, O God, of one blood throughout the earth. Forgive us for not living as sisters and brothers should.

All: **God, have mercy.**

Sister Rosita Shiosee
World Council of Churches

Oh God We Know

A pile of rubbish is set as a focus with people encouraged to look at it during this meditation/intercession. The bigger, the better.
Each stanza and the first two lines of each section could be read by a different reader. The bold type is for congregational response.

Oh God, we know.
We know.

Creator, we know what we do to your creation.
We love it when it is beautiful.
We curse when it is strewn with rubbish.
And we know we waste it as we will.
We know.
In our knowing, we close ourselves to the truth of our actions.
When we can bear to think of our use of what you have made,
We are stunned into inactivity.

Oh Spirit, fire us to move to action.
Burn into our frozen and fearful state.

Oh God, we know.
We know.

Christ, we know what we do to your world.
We love people who treasure your world as you did.
We curse those who abuse the earth on which you stood.
And we know we are among the abusers.
We know.
In our knowing, we turn in on ourselves.
When we can bear to think of our damage to your earth,
We are stunned into inactivity.

Oh Spirit, fire us to move to action.
Burn into our frozen and fearful state.

Oh God, we know.
We know.

Spirit, we know how you live and move in all things.
We love to feel fresh wind and breathe clean air and use them to think of you.
We curse the violent storms and the pungent air of our cities.
And we know we have helped the storms to form and the air to foul.
We know.
In our knowing, we stay where we feel safe.
When we can bear to think of how we have helped shape even the climate,
We are stunned into inactivity.

Oh Spirit, fire us to move to action.
Burn into our frozen and fearful state.

Creator, Christ and Spirit;
One God before time,
One God walking in time,
One God enlivening all time,
Burn into our frozen and fearful state.
Turn us from inside to out;
Liberate us to change our knowing into doing.

In the name of hope,
Amen.

Elizabeth Gray-King
England

Creation

Creation began with light:
light breaking through, spilling out, flooding over,
light giving illumination, warmth and energy,
light drawing life from the earth, stimulating growth.

**Forgive us, Lord, for the way in which we cut off your supply of light to others
by our careless use of energy,
our clouds of pollution and smoke screens of destruction.
Teach us that we block out the light at our peril,
for light is the source of light itself.**

Creation was baptised with water.
Streams and rivers, lakes and seas, brought refreshment and vitality.
Every form of life was filled out and nourished, sustained by moisture.
Rain forests dripped with it,
deserts thirsted for it,
people thrived on it.

Forgive us, Lord, that we are not careful enough with this life-giving source.
Give us a concern for those who try to exist where there is no easy access to water.
Challenge us to support research into the problem
and to care for those who suffer from it.
Teach us that the earth developed its own conservation and distribution system
and we create danger when we disturb the balance of nature.

Creation caught its breath from your Spirit.
The earth filled its lungs with freshness.
People, plants and animals felt the stirring of the breeze.
The wind moved with force and power.

Forgive us, Lord, that we contaminate the air we breathe by our unheeding use of pollutants.
Teach us to be selective and knowledgeable and concerned about the substances we use.
Make us more aware that moving the problem somewhere else is not the right solution.
Creation is sustained by us.
Help us, Lord to be careful keepers of all the life sources you have given to us,
so that your creative processes may be continued in us.

Marjorie Dobson
England

Green Song

When we were young we really didn't care,
We didn't think it was wrong to throw litter everywhere,
The lights and TV we left on,
But now we realise that we were wrong.
We never ever used the re-cycling bins,
We dumped our papers, bottles and tins,
To waste these resources is quite mad,
And now we realise that we were bad.

We went by car and never used our feet,
So traffic jams and pollution clogged up every street,
So take some exercise and breathe fresh air,
Use bike or bus to get you there.
The future of the Earth depends on you and me,
We can't carry on this fantasy,
We must clean up this terrible mess,
Don't cause Mother Nature any stress.

When we were young we really didn't care,
We didn't think it was wrong to throw our litter everywhere.
The lights and the TV we left on,
But now we realise that we were wrong.

Liz Sharma
England

This Is Our Home

Into our hands this precious land is given,
the seas and earth from which all life began,
because of love our cradle was a forest,
the hills and valleys shaped by heaven's plan.
This is our home, the gift of God's creation,
a holy tenure for each varied race,
a place of dreams and fruitful inspiration
where God is seen in every human face.

Here is a harvest fit for all people,
here is a place for everyone on earth,
and here is God revealing all his mysteries,
the power that gave this universe its birth.
This is our home, the gift of God's creation,
soon it will be each child's inheritance,
yet with this knowledge we have found temptation
and now abuse his love's beneficence.

Forgive us Lord, for we have killed your children,
despoiled your planet, poisoned sky and sea,
and worst of all we know what we are doing
but shut our eyes when we don't want to see.
This is our home, the gift of God's creation,
and power grows fat upon the starving bones,
cruel wars destroy the hope of peaceful nations,
and hunger drives our neighbours from their homes.

Help us to use the wisdom you have given,
teach us the way to recreate your land,
and give us grace to share with one another
the richness that is held within our hands.
This is our home, the gift of God's creation,
this is the world God put within our care,
and by his grace we hold the earth's salvation,
the gift of hope for people everywhere.

Tune: Londonderry Air

Colin Ferguson
England

Animals and Plants are Creatures, Too

In America, characteristics of cows and bulls are computerised, the aim being to select seed from the ideal bull for artificial insemination into the ideal cow in order to produce a supercow, generally a Holstein. Before insemination the cow is injected with hormones which ensure a multiple conception. After conception the embryos are flushed out, some are implanted in surrogates, the others frozen, shipped and sold. One 'manager' of a ranch for supercows said of the 'industry' recently on television, 'We're trying to increase everything and keep progress rolling.'

Humans also interfere drastically with plants. In Nebraska, USA, agribusiness drills bore holes for corn irrigation. The dark areas around the holes resemble circles with vegetation reaching skyward. But corn, like English apples, grows best generously spaced where air can circulate during hot days and warm nights. Corn crowded around bore holes requires pesticides to counter diseases. Biotechnicians hope to develop a pesticide-tolerant corn which will flourish in tropical growing conditions and tolerate chemicals which harm the pests but not the plants.

Christian ecologists find this whole procedure disturbing, because humans seem to be interfering in the very nature of fellow creatures, exploiting them for what western economists call economic growth, and 'progress'. A Christian question recurs: Just how far may we go in managing other life on this planet? When does responsible dominion become exploitation? Scripture attests to God's delight in his creatures as they are. The world and all its creatures are God's. 'For every beast of the forest is mine, the cattle on a thousand hills. I know all the birds of the air, and all that moves in the field is mine' (Psalm 50.10-11). There has been a thread within the tradition which maintains the balance between human sharing in creation and our responsibility for other creatures as a cooperative letting be. The 'precautionary principle' is consistent with Christian respect for fellow creatures. Before we interfere with the natures of creatures, before we test GMOs outside on a small island crowded with wild and domesticated life, we first should experiment exhaustively in laboratories. Pope John Paul II endorsed the precautionary principle, with a warning to all of us in our era of scientific and technological hubris. 'If the world of refined technology does not reconcile itself with the simple language of nature in a healthy balance, the life of man will run ever greater risks, of which already we see worrying signs.' (Pope John Paul II)

Above Melrose Abbey in Scotland there is an orchard called Priorwood. One of the apple trees is an Oslin Pippin which was first raised from a pip by the monks at Arbroath and then developed over the centuries by monks in Scotland. The monks grafted fruit trees, planted them, selected, crossed, pruned, thinned and even discarded. This was neither romanticism nor the naive arrogance of today's technical fixers, but responsible dominion in which people both respected and responsibly used fellow living creatures.

Edward P Echlin
England

Water Gets Dirty

Water gets dirty when people and animals misuse the lakes from which drinking water is taken.
To avoid this the following rules must be followed:

1. Do not bathe in lakes meant for drinking water.

2. Do not wash clothes in lakes meant for drinking water.

3. Do not wash animals in lakes.

4. Do not use lakes as toilets.

5. Tanks and sumps in houses should be cleaned from time to time.

A child aged 10
Association for People with Disability
Bangalore, India

Water

God of water pipes and sewerage systems,
we acknowledge that fine words
do not make clean water or reduce infant mortality.
By our efforts to provide water services
where they are needed may we be
the sugar and salt that stops diarrhoea
and gives life a chance.

Janet Lees
England

A Prayer of Confession

There are times when we have nightmares.
We find ourselves haunted by horrors,
        fear filled and frozen.

But we can wake up,
        and see a safer world.

There are some for whom there is no safer world.
Living with them, loving God, must hurt you so deeply,
        for you dream of goodness, peace and joy for all your children,
        and some have only the nightmare.

As we pray for them we come in confession.
Praying for those who live by scavenging like dogs upon a city dump,
        we confess our failure to give everyone the basic stuff of life.
Praying for those who are no more than slaves trapped in ghostly, far-off, factories,
        we confess that our cheap goods have been paid for by their lives.
Praying for those who find the living they scraped together evaporate overnight,
        we confess that our global market place has too many losers.
Praying for those who see their children starving, sick and uneducated,
        we confess that too many nations in debt to us have had to give up too much.
Praying for those who see their land devoured by rising seas,
        we confess that they are paying for our climate-changing greed.

Entering into their nightmare we find ourselves afraid,
        the horrors are so great and the guilt so heavy.

Help us, alongside our confessing,
        to foster hope.
With you, O God, mercy and salvation accompany judgement.
Look on us not simply as we are, but as we long to be.
Look on the world not as we have made it, but as it could be made.
Look on us as your children, and forgive us.
Send us again upon our way to serve and change with the words of Jesus ringing
in our ears:
'Come to me,
all of you who are weary and carry heavy burdens,
and I will give you rest.
Take my yoke upon you.
Let me teach you,
because I am humble and gentle,
and you will find rest for your souls.
For my yoke fits perfectly,
and the burden I give is light.'
Amen.

Neil Thorogood
England

The Earth is the Lord's

Call to Worship

Reader: The earth is the Lord's and the fullness thereof, the world and all that dwells therein.

All: We live in God's world, we are not alone.
We share this life with the heavens and the earth,
with the waters and the land,
with trees and grasses,
with fish, birds and animals,
with creatures of every form and
with all our brothers and sisters.

Reader: God saw all that was made and behold it was very good.

A Hymn celebrating the beauty and mystery of creation

Confession (using different voices)

God's creation is being abused and violated.

We, as human beings, often see ourselves as separate from creation, not woven into the web of life.

The reference to having 'dominion over the earth' is used to exploit and destroy the earth.

As individuals and as societies we become dependent on a lifestyle of limitless growth.

We are quick to blame and judge others rather than accept responsibility for the part that we play in destroying our environment.

We use more than our share of the earth's resources.

We are responsible for massive pollution of earth, water and sky.

We thoughtlessly drop garbage around our homes, schools, churches, places of work and places of play.

Much of the world struggles for survival – good food, clean water, adequate homes.

We squander resources on technologies of destruction – bombs come before bread.

All:	**We are killing the earth:**

Voices:	as mountains of garbage pile up as uranium and nuclear wastes threaten life for centuries to come as we use trees faster than they can re-grow as our precious agricultural land loses its fertility.

All:	**We are killing the waters:**

Voices:	as toxic chemicals and human wastes are dumped into lakes, rivers and oceans as fish and plants die from acid rain as groundwater is poisoned.

All:	**We are killing the skies:**

Voices:	as the global atmosphere heats up from chemical gases as the ozone layer is destroyed as clean air is poisoned by car and truck pollution.

Prayer of Confession

All:	**We confess these sins to you our God, Creator of the universe. You have set before us life and death. Too often we have chosen death.** **We have not loved the earth as you love it.**

Period of Silent Meditation

Assurance of Pardon

Reader:	We know that our God is a God of love as well as of judgement. God promises to be with us as we struggle to be faithful. Thanks be to God.

Prayer for Grace

All:	**Holy and great Creator, we recognise as your people that these problems will not easily be solved. Give us the courage to truly repent and change our ways. May we genuinely ask for forgiveness from you, from the earth and from future generations. May we live this day faithfully loving your creation as you love it. May we walk together toward the future with hope.**

Period of Silent Meditation

The Word

Scriptures

Meditation

Thanksgiving

Voice:	We are thankful for the passion of the children and youth among us who push us to recognise the urgency of the environmental crisis
All:	**Thank you creator and giver of passion**
Voice:	We are thankful for the wisdom of the aged among us who remind us of what it means to respect the earth and to live in community with one another.
All:	**Thank you creator and giver of wisdom.**
Voice:	We are thankful for the insights of the native brothers and sisters among us who draw on their tradition and teach us about the sacredness of all creation and how to live in kinship with it.
All:	**Thank you creator and giver of insight.**
Voice:	We are thankful for the inspiration of those among us who have already begun to live their lives in ways that show a caring for the earth, water and skies.
All:	**Thank you creator and giver of inspiration.**

People may offer their own prayers of thanksgiving.

All:	**We thank you God for all signs of hope that keep us from despairing and point us toward new ways of living.**

Commitment

Reader: We have confessed our part in hurting the earth. We have expressed our thanks for creation and those who care for it. We are ready to commit ourselves to a new way of living. Let us think about the hard questions that can lead to this kind of change:

How do we leave behind the ways that have abused the earth?
How do we show that we care for all creation?
What can we do to stop those whose actions cause great pollution problems?

Period of Silent Meditation

Hymn

Commissioning

Reader: God said; 'I have seen the affliction of my people in Egypt, their loud cry of complaint against their slave drivers I have heard. I know well their suffering.' (Exodus 3:7) In the power of the Spirit go forth, seeing the affliction of the earth as God sees it, hearing creation's cry of complaint as God hears it, knowing its suffering as God knows it.

All: **We commit ourselves anew to seeing the affliction of the earth, hearing its cry and knowing its suffering. We commit ourselves to learning more about the changes that are needed. We commit ourselves to embarking on that long and difficult road toward life in harmony with all God's creatures.**

In covenant with God and with the wisdom of the Holy Spirit we are called to action in the name of Jesus Christ Amen

David Hallman
Canada

A Litany of Praise

Praise God for making all things new,
And for those who work at the art of recreating.

For bottles and cans melted into new life and usefulness,
   Praise be the God of creation renewed!

For paper, once used, made useful again,
   Praise be the God of creation renewed!

For plastic and metal salvaged and recycled,
   Praise be the God of creation renewed!

For car tyres turned into children's play spaces,
   Praise be the God of creation renewed!

For discarded Christmas trees mulching an urban communal garden,
   Praise be the God of creation renewed!

For unwanted computers refurbished and valued somewhere new,
   Praise be the God of creation renewed!

For redundant rifles and mortars sculpted and sold as artworks of hope,
   Praise be the God of creation renewed!

Neil Thorogood
England

Let All Creation Dance and Sing

Do not harm the earth – Revelation 7   Soichi Watanabe

Creator and Sustainer of the Earth

Dear God,
creator and sustainer of the earth
who gave all the fruits of the garden to Adam and Eve on the understanding
that they should not eat from the Tree of Knowledge;
help me to hear your commands, so that, whilst enjoying the fruits of your
abundant creation, I may not plunder the forest,
deny others a fair share of it nor be tempted by the serpent's call to gorge from
our modern equals of the Tree of Knowledge.
Forgive me when I fail to heed your warnings and teach me how to listen more
closely to you. This I ask in your holy name.
Amen

Kevin Fray
England

As Dawn is Breaking in the Sky

As dawn is breaking in the sky
and darkness creeps away,
the world awakes to light and life
and thankful Christians pray,
for God renews our trust again
as night turns into day.

As scars we leave upon the land
are changed again to green,
when nature turns the pages back
with seeds that sleep unseen;
then God renews the earth again
and recreates the scene.

As pain and sorrow, hurt and grief
are touched by Christian care,
which in compassion reaches out
to answer anguished prayer;
then God renews our hope again
by showing love is there.

So let us join to praise the God
who meets our daily needs
and dedicate ourselves again
to Christian words and deeds,
as we renew the vows we made
to follow where Christ leads.

Tune: Sheltered Dale

Marjorie Dobson
England

What a World

Tree of Life

O Tree of Life,
send your roots deep into my life.
Search through the mud of my indifference,
push past the stones of my selfishness;
seek instead the soil of my compassion,
find there the water of my generosity.
O Tree of Life,
draw from me all that I can offer,
to bring buds of hope for the wasted lands,
and leaves for the healing of the nations.

Peter Graystone
England

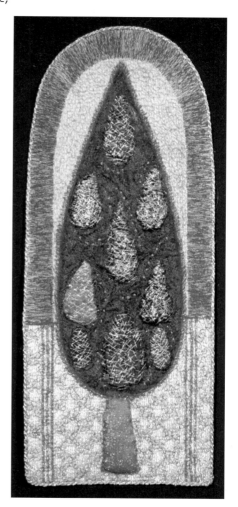

Promising

There is a paleness,
saddening
to reassure,
about the gentle light
spread cautiously
by
earth's half-forgotten sun
now promising
much more
but never less
that these
so slightly
brighter
winter days
when
through the haze
there shines
clear promises
newly renewed
of hoped-for greens
and dazzling scenes
vivid and beautiful.
Yes,
these gentle promises
are no less
no less than wonderful.

David J Harding
England

The Dance of Creation

Lord of the dance …

As the great sea beasts swam the oceans
As the trees spread their branches and brought forth fruit
As the larks filled the sky with song
You looked and saw it was good, and so it was.

As the great sea beasts are hunted towards extinction
As the forests are felled with loss of habitat for many
As the song of the skies is replaced by roar of the jet
We look and sense that all is not good, and so must you.

Help us to recreate heaven on earth
Oceans leaping with life
Land abundant with creeping and crawling
Skies filled with the song of creation
That together we might look and see that it is good, because it is.
Amen

David Pickering
England

Twittering, Leaping, Soaring, Playing

Creating God

Hedges twitter
Whales leap
Eagles soar
Children play
We praise you for the dance of creation.

Hedges grubbed
Oceans silenced
Skies emptied
Children cry
We say sorry for the lament of creation.

Habitats nurtured
Creation respected
Purpose discovered
Your love reflected
Recreation in a new day.

David Pickering
England

Leaping into Spring

Brightly
the morning shines
and
from sun-lighted warmth
amazed
we gazed
across the fields
now even lawns
of
lightly-powdered grass
more white than green
smooth glistening
with lasting temporality
daring
the emerging day
to recreate
another scene
as bright
and comforting.

David J Harding
England

Thus Comes Love

Welcome as spring sun
comes love –
melting the hard ground,
making it possible
for tight-clenched buds
to let go and expand,
to be surprised at their own
evolving growth and purpose.

Consider this gentle healing force,
the sunlight of human relationships.

Cecily Taylor
England

The Hungry Ones

It is good to give a meal
To a very hungry man,
But when he's strong again
And had enough
There are many lasting ways
We can help his future days –
Such as sending a tractor
For his plough, for his plough,
Such as sending a tractor
For his plough.

It is good to give a drink
To a very thirsty mum,
But when she's sipped it all
And had her fill,
There are many lasting ways
We can help her future days –
Such as giving the help to
Dig a well, dig a well,
Such as giving the help to
Dig a well.

It is good to help a child
Who is very keen to learn,
To teach him newer ways
And skills combined;
But a different kind of tool
Is to help provide a school –
And not just feed his body
But his mind, but his mind,
And not just feed his body,
But his mind.

Cecily Taylor
England

Dearest Earth, Our Mother

Dearest Earth, our Mother,
Kind and bountiful:
Loving all your children,
Giving life to all.
We are all your *whanau*
Joined by spiral thread,
Binding all the living,
Linking all the dead.

Earth will live forever
Ancient wisdom said:
Modern wisdom tells us
Earth may soon be dead.
Mother Earth lies bleeding,
Tortured by our hands,
Seeking endless profits
From a finite land.

A-o-te-ro-a,
Sacred island space:
Home where God in nature
Shows a furrowed face;
Land for all our children
Born and yet to be –
May your weeping help us
Long to set you free

William L Wallace
Aotearoa New Zealand

The Voice of Nature

Listen Loved-One! Can't you hear
silences that silence fear,
from the heart of quiet things
singing … speaking … murmurings
of God's Love that echoes through
this Loved World's Peace-Love for you.
As the rocks, plants, seas and skies
symphonise their harmonies
into colour, shape and shade,
all that was and will be made
all that is and is to be
speaks for all for you and me

David J Harding
England

Our Relationship with the Earth

When we seek to capture the earth we take ourselves hostage.

Our relationship with the earth should be organic and symbiotic rather than mechanical, hierarchical and parasitic.

In order to save the earth we need cosmic sensitivity rather than ideological purity.

The primary transaction is not between capital and labour but between human beings and nature. The balance sheet of the earth is even more important for our survival as human beings than the balance sheet of national or global economics.

As the branches are linked to the vine so we are bound together with all other living creatures in the love of God.

William L Wallace
Aotearoa New Zealand

Living Water

Lord of the Harvest,
I thirst for your living water, for I know that without it I may become spiritually dry.
I thirst too for pure water to drink;
for myself and for all people, for without it, we cannot live and to drink dirty water is to risk illness and terrible suffering.
Pour out streams of living water upon the earth
for the sake of my wellbeing and that of my brothers and sisters everywhere.
When people become ill by drinking unsafe water,
grant faith like that of the centurion in Capernaum,
who, speaking for us all, said:
'Lord, my servant lies ill at home but only say the word and my servant shall be healed.'
Amen

Kevin Fray
England

What Better Way?

I love the rain…
(The rain loves me?) …
gently driven
and generously,
answer to
the aridity
of the inanimate
and the thirsts
of the animate;
cleansing, refreshing,
scouring, and powering;
sometimes
bad-tempered and scary,
often withheld
but here sparely.

It's obviously wetting
Is sometimes upsetting.

Too often too sadly
it's unwelcome
and badly maligned,
as if
rain and bad-weather
were bonded together.

A one-way thing
it barely takes.

Nonviolently
it rarely breaks.

Downpour or due
it is sent free!

Yes, of course,
that rain loves me.

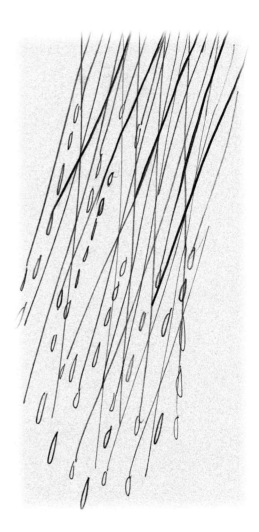

David J Harding
England

Christian Organic Husbandry

The ancient Hindu dictum 'the earth is our mother and we are all her children' is echoed in the Canticle of St Francis praising brother sun and sister moon. St Benedict when at prayer 'saw the whole universe in a single ray of light'. The Buddhist belief in the cycle of life resumes the same theme. For Christians, it is in the humanity of Jesus that the universe finds its centre in all its bodiliness, earthliness and suffering. The spirituality for our time can only be one which seeks to heal and reconcile all living things where the natural world is not interfered with by pollution, abuse or chemicals in Christ, who was raised in glory for the whole of creation. This is the spiritual basis of Christian organic husbandry.

For the organic grower the presence of the earthworm in the soil means health and vitality. People sustained by the produce of this soil are more likely to be healthy people. When the finely tuned balance of the dynamism inherent in creation continues to enhance life in all its variety. The human person has a vital part to play in the enhancement. Created in the likeness and image of God he/she has a nurturing, sustaining and life-giving role, to perfect the work of creation according to its own laws and integrity.

At Minster Abbey, Kent, England, farming has grown since the 1930s when the founding sister arrived from Bavaria to re-introduce monastic life to Minster. The sisters started to earn their living through the only way they knew, that of farming. It was their deep faith and trust in God's providence that they grew fruit and vegetables and fodder for livestock.

Farming was partly organic and partly with chemicals but now they have ceased to use them. Herbs and wild plants have reappeared in the grassland which benefit the sheep and goats. The deep roots of the plants bring up valuable minerals and the flowers attract butterflies and insects which have their own important part to play in the eco-system. Forty native trees give food and shelter to birds and other wildlife. Vegetables and fruit are nourished by compost and farm manure, giving them strength to withstand disease and produce healthy food.

There are many different approaches to ecological gardening but its main aim is the establishment of a rich and varied habitat sustaining a healthy soil through composing organic waste and using natural materials rather than chemicals. Working with the natural environment can be a continued voyage of discovery. This is possible in a window box or on a few hundred acres, in the city or in the countryside and brings a wholeness and joy to our lives.

Ancilla Dent OSB
adapted by Geoffrey Duncan

The LOAF Principles

Food matters. The kind of food we choose demonstrates our care for God's creation. What food is provided in our church? At home? How far did it travel?

Christian Ecology Link asks people to use their LOAF and follow one or more of the LOAF principles when planning any communal meal like a Harvest Celebration, Alpha Supper or regular church meal.

Locally produced food means shorter journeys for farm animals to markets and abattoirs, less climate damaging food miles, less lorry traffic, less demand for new roads, support for the local economy and local farmers, and regional variety.

Organically grown food avoids the use of synthetic pesticides and herbicides. Organic cultivation leads to a healthier soil with more organic material, micro-organisms and other wildlife, and no genetically engineered organisms released into the countryside.

Animal friendly means that our fellow creatures, under God, are treated humanely. Those still eating food produced from animals can choose organic, or free range, meat and eggs. Organically reared animals are subject to strict welfare regulation.

Fairly traded coffee, tea, and other foods which have to be imported, ensure that workers who produce the food get a fair wage. Farmers in the UK also need a fair price for their produce.

A loaf of bread is the staple food for many people. Bread has symbolic meaning for Christians. Jesus blessed and broke bread and gave it to his disciples saying, 'Do this in remembrance of me.' In St John's Gospel Jesus is described as 'The Bread of Life'. Christian Ecology Link asks you to use your LOAF to make a difference.

Barbara Echlin
England

Aammiq: A Special Place
(A Rocha's Project)

The Aammiq wetlands are a very special conservation site. 200 hectares of reed bed, pools and seasonally flooded pasture set in about twenty square kilometres of environmentally valuable fields, hillside and woodland at an altitude of nearly 900 metres in Lebanon's Bekaa Valley, they are a special place in many different ways.

Aammiq's setting is special. To the west, over the towering limestone mass of Mount Lebanon, the waters of the Mediterranean are just twenty miles away. But only fifty miles to the east, across the Bekaa and beyond the bare slopes of the Anti-Lebanon range, lies the edge of the vast, and advancing, Arabian desert. Aammiq's wetlands are a threatened outpost of water in an increasingly arid region.

Aammiq's wildlife is special. Because of the water, the wetlands, the adjacent fields and the hillside slopes are a haven for plants, birds and animals throughout the year. Many of these species are poorly known and many have a high ecological significance. But Aammiq's most spectacular wildlife feature and something that gives it an international environmental value, is the passage of millions of birds over it on their yearly migrations between Africa and Europe. For some birds the Bekaa is simply a pathway that allows them to avoid flying over the heights of Mount Lebanon. For others, Aammiq itself is a vital stop-over, a chance for food, water and rest on this dry, barren and dangerous leg of a long journey.

Aammiq's history is special. As one of the premier environmental sites in Lebanon, Aammiq is one of the last remaining fragments of an environmental splendour that the Old Testament writers praised as similar to that of the Garden of Eden. The many ruins and fortifications in the area are reminders of another aspect of history; every regional superpower from the earliest times onwards has advanced and retreated past Aammiq.

Aammiq feels special, when in winter, the black storm clouds drape the mountains and the bitter gusts lash the dark waters of the pools. It feels special in early spring when, with the snows of Mount Hermon gleaming against perfect blue skies, life returns to the reed beds and the first clouds of migrating birds drift northwards. It feels special in late spring when marsh harriers glide lazily over the reed beds that are alive with the chaotic murmurings, chatterings and croakings of new life. It feels special when, in the hot days of summer, you sit gratefully under the shade of the trees squinting out into the hot and dusty air aware that the desert is very close. And when you have just come from the smoggy, congested air of Beirut, Aammiq feels very special indeed. Also, Aammiq is a very special conservation site. There is much about Aammiq that is typical of so many of the world's threatened environments. The list of hazards that have afflicted and may still afflict Aammiq are: deforestation, fertiliser pollution, fires, hunting, over-pumping of water for agriculture, overgrazing, pesticide abuse, quarrying, road widening and war. If the threats Aammiq faces are diverse and complex so are the difficulties faced in preserving it. Preservation requires simultaneously balancing the competing demands of environmentalists, landowners, tenant farmers, migrant workers and tourists, as well as juggling various legal and economic factors at local, national and international levels. Everything has to be done within a society that is still painfully rebuilding itself after a long series of bitter internal and external conflicts.

A Rocha's Aammiq Project has three interlocking aspects; education, conservation and scientific study. All three have impressive achievements and exciting goals for the future. In education, A Rocha has the only field studies centre in Lebanon and provides teaching for school parties and training for teachers. In conservation, the marsh habitats have been preserved and enhanced so that despite three dry winters the marsh is now more extensive than for several decades. In science, A Rocha has accumulated a large amount of scientific data on the Aammiq area and its environs. The complexities, difficulties and uncertainties of working in Aammiq should not be underestimated. Nevertheless, the results have been remarkable. Aammiq is a special place and so is the project to save it.

Chris Walley
England/Wales

A Song of God's Goodness

Creator God, you made this wondrous earth
and filled it with the creatures of your choice:
all look in hope to you, who gave them birth,
and all together praise you and rejoice.

In all the oceans and the seas they play,
in fields and deserts creep and walk and run;
birds fill the air, their song greets each new day;
all creatures have their homes beneath the sun.

We too, like these, are creatures of your grace;
you send us grain for bread and grapes for wine;
in all you give your generous love we trace
and know that all Creation is divine.

Until the end of time we'll sing our praise
to you, the Source and End of all that lives,
give thanks for the delight that fills our days
and all the strength and hope your Spirit gives.

Tune: Chilton Foliat

William Whitson
England

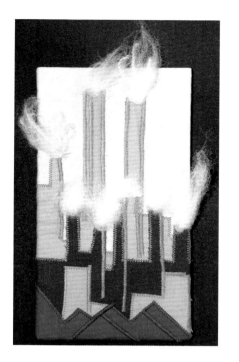

A Litany for Eco-justice

Because many refuse to acknowledge that the earth is a living, interrelated system ...

All: **We must cry out for eco-justice.**

Because fertile earth has been converted into landfills, forests into deserts, running rivers into silted floodplains ...

All: **We must cry out for eco-justice.**

Because grave assaults on the biosphere – acid rain, desertification, waste accumulation, overpopulation, ozone depletion – rob us all of our heritage ...

All: **We must cry out for eco-justice.**

Because governments and corporations play off economic and environmental concerns against each other ...

All: **We must cry out for eco-justice.**

Because industrial countries persist in lifestyles, policies and production methods which endanger human existence and the rest of the world ...

All: **We must cry out for eco-justice.**

Because many use power to dominate humans and nature ...

All: **We must cry out for eco-justice.**

Because materialism leaves a spiritual vacuum, an alienation that is pervasive where people have grown isolated from nature and from each other ...

All: **We must cry out for eco-justice.**

Because we have forgotten our rootedness in an integrated way of life ...

All: **We must cry out for eco-justice.**

Because vast areas have been rendered unfit for habitation by native plants and animals and are now becoming unfit for human habitation as well ...

All: **We must cry out for eco-justice.**

Because the degradation of agricultural land is the most widespread threat to human life world-wide ...

All: We must cry out for eco-justice.

Because, while more land is rendered uninhabitable each year, more people are added to the world's population …

All: We must cry out for eco-justice.

Because some species are endangered and even extinct as a result of destroyed habitats …

All: We must cry out for eco-justice.

Because many commercial products are tested on animals in painful ways …

All: We must cry out for eco-justice.

Because deforestation displaces indigenous peoples; hazardous waste sites are located near poor neighbourhoods; industrialized factory farms eliminate the small family farmer; and international policies of free trade hurt many people and the earth …

All: We must cry out for eco-justice.

Because each form of life is integrated with every other form of life, and because we have not rallied to the earth's defense.

All: We must cry out for eco-justice.

Diann Neu
USA

A Prayer of Intercession

God of earth and sea and sky,
>> creator and sustainer of all,
>>> your invitation is that we work with you
>>>> to tend and nurture all that you have made.

In obedience and hope we come with our prayers for your people and your world.

We pray for all who work with creation:
>> for farmers and fishers,
>> for harvesters and miners,
>> for shippers and sellers,
>> for conservers and restorers.

We pray for all who struggle for creation:
>> for campaigners and reporters,
>> for researchers and publishers,
>> for whistle-blowers and protestors,
>> for shoppers and decision-makers.

We pray for all who delve into creation:
>> for experimenters and collectors,
>> for curators and breeders,
>> for explorers and photographers,
>> for programme-makers and presenters.

We pray for all who celebrate creation:
>> for composers and painters,
>> for writers and sculptors,
>> for potters and gardeners,
>> for walkers and divers.

We pray for all who hurt creation:
>> for exploiters and smugglers,
>> for abusers and dealers,
>> for poisoners and polluters
>> for wreckers and destroyers.

Dear Lord of all creation,
>> you have entrusted a world into our fragile, uncertain hands.
Help us to work wisely and without tiring for the good of your creation
>> and all of its creatures.
Help us to challenge and change whatever harms and destroys.
We offer our prayers in the name of Jesus Christ our Lord,
>> and through the power of your Holy Spirit.
Amen.

Neil Thorogood
England

A Prayer of Praise and Thanksgiving

Aren't you too extravagant, Lord?
Creation is so full of life,
      resources so abundant,
            beauty so overwhelming.

Aren't you too reckless, Lord?
Life is so fragile,
      humanity so powerful,
            disaster so possible.

Aren't you too trusting, Lord?
Letting us nurture,
      permitting our tampering,
            risking our mistakes.

Extravagant, reckless and trusting God,
      we worship you and adore you.
May we never cease to worship.
May your trust be vindicated through our actions,
      your recklessness be repaid through our faithfulness,
            your extravagance be shared through our generosity.
So may we be true disciples of Jesus.
Amen.

Neil Thorogood
England

A Litany Of Hope

      God has given us a good home,
All: **Here on this Earth that we share.**

      God has blessed us with riches,
All: **In the beauty and abundance of creation.**

      God has forged for us a family,
All: **Through the marvellous variety of humanity.**

      God has offered us a mission,
All: **In the caring that we share.**

      God has challenged us to serve,
All: **Through Bible-word and word-made-flesh.**

Neil Thorogood
England

Out of the Ark

Floodwaters ending:
Noah feels hopeful.
Soon he'll be sending
out his grey dove.
Back she comes flying
to the ark, peaceful;
her beak supplying
one moss-green leaf.

Floodwaters dropping:
Noah is thankful.
God must be stopping
grim work as judge.
High sweeps the rainbow,
Noah is joyful!
Harvests again grow,
blessing not drudge.

Once more creation
lives with a promise,
tastes God's salvation,
shoulders a task.
This world's a garden,
yielding fresh produce;
yet every Eden
duties will ask.

Are we respectful
of earth's resources?
Are we neglectful
of what God lends?
God looks for servers,
trustworthy stewards
counting the silver
he or she spends.

Like Jonah steering
into the distance,
gradually nearing
mountain top mark:
if we are ready,
challenge awaits us
as we climb steady
out of the ark.

Tune: Bunessan

Look at the birds of the air - Matthew 6: 26
Soichi Watanabe

David Mowbray
England

Longdendale Psalm

The Longdendale Trail, in the Peak District National Park, UK part of the national cycle network runs along the Longdendale Valley, the line of the former Manchester to Sheffield railway line.

God is like a shepherd,
therefore, I will continue to take risks.
Before me is this long green valley
whose reservoirs of abundant water refresh me.
God's presence with me is
as awesome as this straight path which takes me home.
In bad weather this valley can be as dark as death,
yet God is my companion even in my fears,
with me like a survival blanket in my backpack.
There's a feast here of flowers, fruit and fungi
and it's a joy to walk this way,
watching reservoirs gradually fill up again.
God, creative lover and companion,
with me in the everyday things:
I'll be at home with you forever.

Janet Lees
England

The Healing Power of Bamboo

Bamboo is presumed to have originated in Asia. This perennial tree grows to a height of twelve metres with its trunk eight to fifteen centimetres in diameter. It grows wild, in clusters, throughout most parts of India, especially in the hilly forests of western and southern India but is cultivated only in the lower Himalayas and in the valleys of the Ganges and Indus. Every year between July and October, new shoots sprout at the base of the tree.

The leaves of the bamboo tree are stimulant, aromatic and tonic but do not have any prominent taste. The leaves and young shoots of bamboo are beneficial in the treatment of stomach troubles and in many parts of India they are used to treat diarrhoea.

The tender shoots are useful in the treatment of respiratory diseases and a prescription for the shoots should be taken with a tablespoon of honey once or twice daily.

They are useful to arrest bleeding.

Anil Kumar Patil
south India

The Healing Power of Red Gum Tree

This tree is also known as Blue Gum Tree or Stringy Bark Tree.
The leaves are leathery in texture, hang obliquely or vertically, and are studded with glands containing a fragrant, volatile oil. The flowers when in bud are covered with a cup-like membrane which is thrown off as a lid when the flower expands. The fruit is surrounded by a woody, cup shaped receptacle and contains numerous minute seeds.

Eucalyptus trees are quick growers and many species reach a great height. *Eucalyptus amygdalin* (Labille) is the tallest known tree and specimens attain as much as 480 feet, exceeding in height even the Californian Big Tree (*Sequoia gigantea*).

It is a stimulant, antiseptic and aromatic. Many species yield valuable timber and various oils. Eucalyptus Oil is used as a stimulant and antiseptic gargle. It increases cardiac action and its properties confer some anti-malarial action

The medicinal Eucalyptus Oil is probably the most powerful antiseptic of its class, especially when it is old, as ozone is formed on exposure to the air. It has a disinfectant action, destroying the lower forms of life and for parasitic skin infections.

An emulsion made by shaking up equal parts of the oil and powdered gum-arabic with water has been given internally in small doses for pulmonary tuberculosis and other microbiotic diseases of the lungs and bronchitis. In croup and spasmodic throat troubles, the oil may be freely applied, externally.

In veterinary practice, Eucalyptus Oil is administered to horses with influenza, to dogs with distemper and to all animals with septicaemia.

Anil Kumar Patil
south India

The Gum Trees

I look out of my window at gum trees, the eucalypts of Australia, in great variety; tough trees for a harsh world. They are not glossy, bright green but a muted olive grey-green. Many have only a thin crown of foliage and shed more leaves in a drought. Some have tall straight trunks so that you feel you are in a forest of telegraph poles. Others, particularly the angophoras, have wonderfully twisted trunks and branches, not one metre, going straight. Many shed bark each year, untidily, in slabs or strips. There are smooth grey trunks that look polished and some that glisten after rain with bronze beauty. In the summer the flowers are cream or pink, high up there to face the sun. The fallen leaves are hard and crackle underfoot, their oil bleached out of them. The timber is tough for my handsaw and not meant for the delicate trades.

Just one part of the flora of one part of the world, toughened through millennia, clothing the old and thin soils of Australia. If, then, God so clothes the earth will there not be care for you, children of Australia?

Bernard Thorogood
Australia

The Rubber Tree

The classic Rubber Tree, Rubber Plant or India Rubber Plant is native to India and Malaysia, The *elastica* is among the oldest plant used as a houseplant, world-wide.

Elastica leaves, stems and even wood 'bleed' white sticky sap, when broken or damaged, from which rubber can be made. Some people are allergic to this sap when it is applied to their skin.

This is a large tree, growing to forty - fifty feet tall and even wider with its spreading branches held up by aerial roots, which become multiple trunks.

The South Florida native, commonly called 'Strangler Fig' is a huge tree of up to fifty feet. Strangler Fig grows like a vine when young, often germinating in trees and in palm fibbers or fronds. Birds distribute seeds, which will sprout almost anywhere and without soil. It is their aerial roots that surround its victims and over time kills its host with its size.

As a houseplant, a variety of rubber plant is very popular. It is able to adapt to and endure lower light conditions and generally poor treatment. It needs a lot of light and should be kept away from cold and drafts in winter. The soil should be kept lightly to moderately moist with good drainage. Most soils will be fine and largely sandy soils mixed with some organics are ideal. Light fertilization is best. A small young plant should adapt to home conditions quickly and easily. Larger plants most often have a temporary decline with much shedding and/or browning of the leaves which causes concern to their owners.

Anil Kumar Patil
south India

A New Heaven and A New Earth

One can understand why we are promised a new earth. But why a new heaven? The answer has to do with the fact that in biblical times heaven or the sky was thought of as a dome protecting the earth (Genesis 1: 6 – 7; Job 37: 18). Fixed into the dome were the stars, the sun and moon, which were understood as determining the seasons and festivals (Genesis 1: 6 – 7, 14 – 18). Therefore having a new earth meant a new heaven to regulate its life. The focus is on the earth. The Book of Revelation is too often believed to be concerned with heaven. Everything moves towards a new earth which will replace the present injustice-ridden and blood-drenched earth.

What those who risk their lives in witnessing to truth and justice are promised is not an escape into a heavenly world but life on a renewed earth. They are not taken up into the New Jerusalem; it comes down to them. It is planted firmly upon this earth. It is no exaggeration to say that the whole point of John's writing his book is to impress upon his readers the fact that it is *this* world which is the place where God's righteousness will triumph.

How we are to envisage the new earth defies imagination. Like much else in Revelation, it is metaphor; but what it stands for is of the greatest possible significance in determining the values by which Christians are to live and to which they are called to bear witness. It does not provide us with answers to the vexing social and political questions of our times but by showing us that the material world is of fundamental importance to God it does indicate that finding answers to such questions should occupy us.

R J McKelvey
England

The Meeting

Where were you, Lord?
We called the meeting,
for Monday evening
the 26th June.
All members were there,
except you.
Where were you, Lord?
I went to speak and lost my thread,
I couldn't think,
what sounded good in my head,
as words came out,
they came out dead.
Our bodies sat on boring chairs,
our faces looked into each others,
and saw nothing real.
That's how I knew you weren't there.
I was stiff, dumb,
and seemed stuck to my chair.

My child, I couldn't make the meeting.
I was at an opening,
the petals of a garden daisy,
and an evening enjoying the fragrance
of the night scented stock.
I was in the evening breeze
that called my heart to be,
a cooling on my heated world.
In the rain, the sheet lightning, I sent
through the committee of nature's elements.
I roared away my wrath in the thunder.

Where were you child?
I was waiting in the moment.
in the flowers and the trees
and the poppy's head
that would not break,
in the storm I sent
nor let its colour run,
and turn the green grass red.
In the laughing from my belly
and the weeping from my heart.
In the beauty and the brokenness
of the world I love.
Have I got your attention, child
Can we start?
Can we start?

Pat Randall
England

Living Waterways

Living Waterways, is located in Southall and Hayes, West London, UK. In a heavily built up multi-cultural area the project aims to open up the wonders of creation to people who have little chance to go to natural areas and see the beauty of God's creation at first hand.

The Revd Dave Bookless, (A Rocha's UK Director) has been working full-time on the project since February 2001, and has already built up a team of enthusiastic volunteers and qualified staff, including an administrator, a scientific officer and two environmental education officers. He says: 'It's been a challenging but rewarding first year, working in the community with lots of different organisations, I have found there have been far more opportunities to talk to people about what motivates me as a Christian than I ever had as a local vicar'.

Some highlights include:

- Through A Rocha's campaigning, a 90 acre wasteland site on the edge of Southall is going to be turned into a Country Park and Nature Conservation Area by the local council. A Rocha Living Waterways provided the ecological impact assessment for this, and co-ordinated working parties to clear up rubbish. The site, formerly full of burnt-out cars, fly-tipped waste and illegal motorbike scrambling, will now contain nature trails, areas of open green space, and a children's playground.

- Over 90 species of bird on or over the site, and more than 20 species of butterfly, making this the most important unprotected wildlife area in West London. A Rocha hope to have a long-term input into the management of this area.

- Two environmental play schemes have been organised for 80 children, along with after-school clubs in local schools, an environmental poster competition for children, and helping to create a Wildlife Learning Garden in a local primary school are all a part of the project.

- A local Asian businessman donated a new eco-car, a dual-fuel, Toyota Prius for the project work, and to help spread the message of why Christians should be involved in practical environmental action.

- Two Environment Education Officers with funding for three years. Their work will involve working in local schools, after-school clubs and play schemes, and from 2003, taking groups on a Floating Classroom on the Grand Union Canal.

The Bishop of London has said : 'I believe that environmental issues are amongst the most urgent we face in this new century, and it is imperative that Christians are in the forefront of debate and practical action. A Rocha's proposal for an urban environmental project in multiracial London is an important Christian initiative, which I warmly endorse and personally support'.

The vision of A Rocha Living Waterways is to be a catalyst in helping the local communities to understand, respect and enjoy the local environment, and to bring very different people together in this. As a Christian organisation, they have been welcomed by other-faith leaders in Southall, where creation is seen as an opportunity for building on shared values.

Dave Bookless
England

Global Perspectives

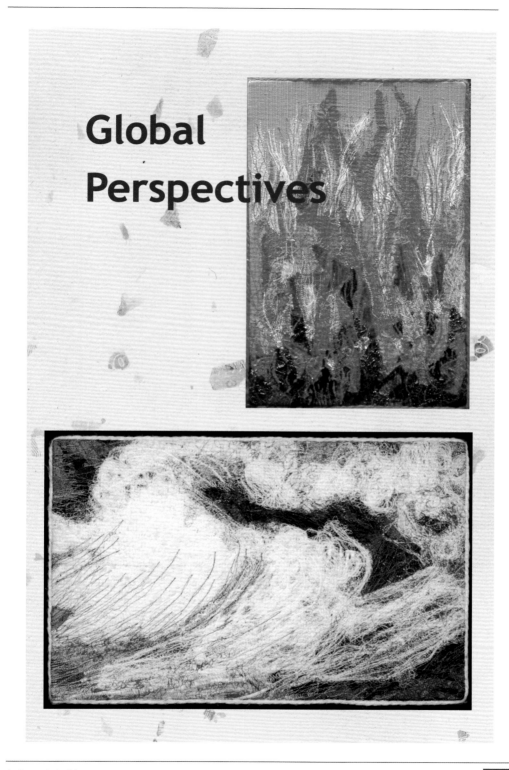

In the Beginning ...

In the beginning your spirit moved and ...

light shone,
oceans gathered,
earth yielded,
seasons ordered,
waters teemed,
animals multiplied,
your image reflected

and creation rejoiced in wonder.

Through poor stewardship humanity is ...

overshadowing creation
warming oceans
soiling earth
changing climate
polluting waters
extinguishing species
scarring your image

and creation groans in turmoil.

May your spirit move again across the depths to ...

Enlighten world leaders
to act for the environment
Empower churches
to be stewards of creation
Encourage each one of us
to care for your gifts through our lives.
Amen

David Pickering
England

Tread Gently

Blessed are you who tread gently on the earth
      for you will be part of the new creation.
Blessed are you who share its resources now
      for you will also share in the feast prepared for all people.
Blessed are you who weep at the destruction of the land
      for you will laugh and dance in green fields.
Blessed are you when you are hated and insulted
      because you show up the folly of others
      who do not share your concern for the earth and its people.
      Rejoice in that day and leap for joy because you shall dwell with God.

But woe to you who exploit the earth,
      for you have already received your comfort.
Woe to you who are greedy and ensure your own wants are met
      without a thought for the toil of others
      for you will go hungry.
Woe to you who laugh as factories pump waste into rivers,
      as exhaust fumes fill the skies,
      As unprotected workers inhale pesticides,
      for you will mourn and weep.
Woe to you when bankers and shareholders speak well of your profits
      and ignore your ethics,
      for the Lord knows the secrets of the heart.

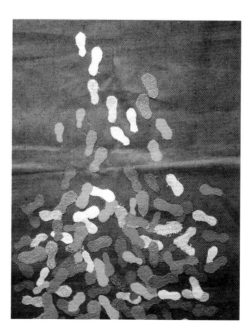

Jenny Spouge
England

Earthspin

The earth spins round the sun, the moon spins round the earth.
All living things are circling from the moment of their birth.
Some lands are desert, while some lands flood.
Some people live in plenty while others have no food.

Keep the forest green, there is life within its heart.
In earth's eco-system, everything plays its part.
Keep the forest green with its canopy of shade,
Its roots hold the earth beneath the glade.

Repeat: The earth spins round the sun ...

Keep the oceans clean, let the crystal rivers flow,
All life came from water, millions of years ago.
Every bubbling stream, every lake and waterfall,
Ensures life continues for us all.

Repeat: The earth spins round the sun ...

Liz Sharma
England

Creation Seen - Creation Unseen

Let all that is visible worship the Lord:
High mountain ranges and leaves on the tree.
Microscopic creatures, sky-scraping towers,
Cascading waters and stars in the sky,
Colours of the rainbow, people of the nations,
Lightning and landscape, sunset and shadow,
Greatly give praise to the One who created you.

Let all that's invisible worship the Lord:
Life-giving oxygen, cool of the breeze,
Electrical current and radio waves,
Scent of the flower and taste on the tongue,
Burning emotion, mysterious sleep,
Silence and gravity, music and laughter,
Greatly give praise to the One who created you.

Peter Graystone
England

Deep in the Core of the Earth

Deep in the core of the earth,
primeval forces flow,
their cycles ever pressing on
unseen, alive, below.

Here on the planet's face
is birth and life and death,
the seasons ever rolling on
with every fleeting breath.

Far in the skies beyond
the stars and planets turn,
their every movement set in space,
each with its time to burn.

God of the worlds which you made,
we offer praise and prayer,
with human need for faith and trust,
and confidence to share.

That all the work we do
will harvest in your name –
while life develops, changes, turns,
your love remains the same.

Heather Phillips
England

Healing Creation

Word of God, in the beginning you spoke and ...

Oceans teemed
Earth blossomed
Creatures flourished
Heavens sang

Through time we have responded ...

Utilising water
Cultivating earth
Naming creatures
Exploring heavens

But in greed and folly we have also ...

Fouled oceans
Scarred earth
Harmed creatures
Obscured heaven

At this time of opportunity we pray that you may ...

Give leaders wisdom
Inspire your church
Enthuse disciples
To heal your creation.

David Pickering
England

Ecological Footprints

Creator God,
we know that our *ecological footprints* –
the area of the world's surface required
to sustain us – are growing unsustainably.
We take up more land as others lose it.
We build our own wealth to the detriment of
others and impoverish generations to come.

Your way is for us to share and to reduce the
harm we inflict on others – seen and unseen.
You would have us build up the 'common ground'
and pursue all that makes for peace.

Therefore teach us to walk lightly on this earth,
that our every step may be as a gentle footprint
for those who follow; that our tracks be healthy
guides for all life; and that our impact on the
planet leaves hope for the future.
Amen

Martyn Goss
England

All You Powerful Things, Praise the Lord

All you powerful things praise the Lord:
Niagara Falls and Pacific Ocean,
Tiger and tyrannosaurus,
Killer whale and golden eagle,
Forces of gravity and pull of the tide,
Forked lightning and shout of the throng;
Praise and magnify the one who created you.

All you weak things praise the Lord:
Sparkle of light and breath of the breeze,
Scuttling ant and wriggling tadpole,
Tear in the eye and hair on the head,
Soft feathers and gentle sighs,
Scent of the rose and whisper of prayer;
Praise and magnify the one who created you.

Peter Graystone
England

What A World

What an extraordinary world is this creation,
more wonderful than our imagination can conceive;
full of surprising forms of life and sudden beauties,
secret colours and interlocking destinies.
We could not manufacture a single rose bud
or blow a cloud across the sky.

Yet it is such a cruel world.
The floods sweep across Orissa,
the tornado batters the poor in the Philippines,
drought wearies the farming families of the Sudan,
and disease lurks where mosquitoes flourish.

The cycle of life seems cruel,
so utterly without sentiment,
a food chain without end
where survival is the absolute priority for all.

Your world, Creator God, so lovely and so cruel
is a dangerous mixture.
It is life:
endless possibility, exploding diversity,
and a world whose destiny we cannot see.
May we not add to the cruelty with our
human longing for power
till the whole structure tips over,
but move the balance towards fairness
and relief and neighbourhood,
towards creativity and health
because we love life and life's eternal hope.

Bernard Thorogood
Australia

With Her Rucksack on Her Back

Awamma is eighteen years old and lives in Jalahalli village which is situated in a very remote part of northern Karnataka state in south India. She contracted the polio virus at the age of two and was left with total paralysis in both her legs. She and her family had no access to any rehabilitation services, so her disability worsened as she developed severe contractures in her legs and hips. She was unable to go to school since she could not walk the two kilometres there and back.

When she was sixteen years old, Awamma heard about Samarthya, a Community Based Rehabilitation Programme for People with Disabilities, which provides services in her part of Karnataka State. This proved to be the turning point in her young life. Through Samarthya, Awamma underwent surgery and extensive physiotherapy and is now able to walk confidently with the aid of her calipers and crutches.

These days, she thinks nothing of putting her rucksack on her back and making the long walk to and from her high school every day.

Ruth Duncan
England/south India

Walking tall

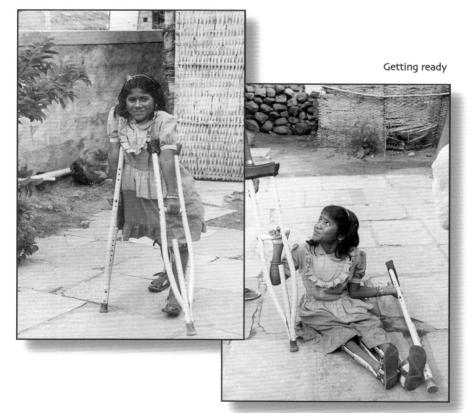

Getting ready

Bring Resurrection

God of the Springtime bulbs and the lengthening days,
we look to you for new life;
bring resurrection to this wakening country.

God of the war-torn lands and the needy men and women,
we look to you for new life;
bring resurrection to a changing Afghanistan.

God of the unyielding volcano and the frightened people,
we look to you for new life;
bring resurrection to a ravaged Goma.

God of the floods and the fields and the farmers,
we look to you for new life;
bring resurrection to a vulnerable Mozambique.

God of the rich and God of the poor,
we look to you for new life;
bring Easter to all this weary world.

Peter Graystone
England

The Wisdom of the Chipmunk

Did you see the chipmunk
this morning carrying the bread?
The bread was cut and jellied
just for him.

We met – he stopped
to see what I would do
he really checked me out

we looked and stared
at first he was quite scared
then with courage he took his bread
and proudly walked away

when I am frightened
like this little one
I must be patient, watch and listen,
hold the feeling

until 'wisdom' breaks through
to encourage me
throughout life's journey.

Eleanore Milardo
USA

A Prayer from A Psychiatric Environment

Lord,
It is peaceful here when everybody's quiet.
This window always seems to get the sun in the morning.
I'm looking at a caterpillar, one of those furry ones
Crawling along the pussy willow someone brought in from outside
To put in the bronze vase on the little table here in the window
(probably a visitor or one of the patients who has got her clothes back)
I'm watching it crawl along its branch, quarter-inch by quarter-inch
It crawls very slowly. I crawl slowly too.

Outside the window, there in the sunshine, there's a bird singing,
Looking for its breakfast. Perhaps it's a skylark
(do skylarks sing when they're hungry?
Do skylarks sing at all?)
Perhaps my caterpillar can hear it, if caterpillars can hear.
He's safer here.
Here in the ward, on his twig, he's safe.

It's a beautiful world you have made, Lord, but it can be a cruel one.
You know that, don't you?
No-one better than you!
You know that sometimes we need a bit of quietness,
A bit of safety.
Thank you, Lord, for giving me somewhere to stay.
Somewhere to hide until I'm a bit better and can face the world again.
I will go out again, I promise, when the time comes
But until then –
Keep me, O Lord, as the apple of an eye
Hide me under the shadow of your wings.

Roger Grainger
England

It Is Not Fair

It is not fair
to breathe clean air
when others choke
and gasp and writhe
polluted by the transport stuff
we need to stay alive.

It is not fun
clearly to see
when others blunder
neither learning to be blind
nor recognising well
their incapacity.

It is not fair
to tell the truth
when others lie
deceived and unaware
that they act out
a monstrous unreality.

It is not fun
to feel the hurt
when others damage
senseless of the damaging
they take upon themselves
as well as give.

It is not fair
to live in peace
when others war
with peaceless means
that must ensure
continued violencing.

It is not fate
that we must love
while others hate
ignore or hurt
the unloved victims
of their carelessness.

It is so good
that there is
Love and Joy and Peace
for each and all
in and beyond
such calvaried be-bashedness.

David J Harding
England

Desert Landscape with Nomads

An expatriate family driving across Rajasthan, north India, avoids the tourist route and takes the ancient highway.

Suddenly, sky-high cumulous pillars of dust block out every landmark – it seems even the present century.
A drum-roll of hoof beats, first distant, increases in intensity. From the dimness emerges a legion of pastoral people and their livestock, creatures mutely questioning the ground for survival. The cacophany of bleating, the jangle of bells, the acrid animal scents assault the foreign travellers.

The brightness in the herdsmen's eyes is an astonishment – not found in city dwellers, east or west.
A sinewy elder approaches. He wields his staff with the authority of a patriarchal. A woman comes alongside. In a red and yellow swinging skirt, she could be the prototype gypsy. Her whiplash stride keeps pace with her laden camel. She pauses beside the halted car. The donkey she drives carries her two small sons, packed among rugs. The newest long-eared lambs and kids lurch in the saddlebags where cooking pots are strung.

Clearly the woman pities the boys trapped in the low Mercedes so she throws out a challenge – 'Let your sons ride more fittingly!' She indicates her camel, gaudy with tasselled hangings.

The foreign woman understands and nods. She musters her best Hindi. 'Good thing. But only if your sons will join our humble carriage.' The camel kneels, grumbling protest. After exchange of hostages it again sways to its feet. The herder's children, uneasy behind glass, clearly feel they have the worse bargain. A few miles on, the families regroup, feeling inter-cultural bonding. They take their separate ways.

The herders, with need of water deep in their bones as marrow, must face a life-long quest for sustenance, for humans and for beasts. This is the Abraham syndrome, the beckoning far horizons, life's precarious hurl towards merest survival. Failure spells death. The westerners take home a trophy shot – their children ride a camel.

Grace Westerduin
England

Bushmen

The 'Bushmen', the first inhabitants of southern Africa, have suffered colonisation and oppression from Bantu and later European invaders for over a thousand years. Those in Botswana are still discriminated against, and face a government which wishes to evict many of them from their ancestral homelands in the Central Kalahari Game Reserve. *Survival* has supported the Bushmen for many years.

In late 1999, the BBC broadcast a *Survival* appeal focussing on the Khwe Bushman in the Reserve and we issued a bulletin in Setswana as well as our usual languages. The Botswana government replied to many *Survival* supporters who wrote, but did not answer the real concerns: the Bushmen's ownership rights over – and right to remain on – their ancestral land. *Survival* continues to pressure the government in Botswana and its representatives in Europe and is ensuring the case attracts press attention.

Guidelines issued in Botswana in 2000 recognised, encouragingly, that Bushmen will remain on their land but tried to limit hunting further and still ignored land ownership. Later, some wildlife officials beat up people in a Bushman village in the reserve for alleged over-hunting and tortured some of the them for several days. *Survival* protested to the Botswana government and interviewed the victims.

Apart from their hunting and land rights, the Bushmen in the Reserve are most concerned about water. They currently rely on a bore-hole in one of their villages from which water is trucked by the council to other Bushmen communities. This supply is not really sufficient for their needs and can be unreliable. *Survival* is supporting their negotiations with the authorities over improving the water supply.

Families who resist eviction are determined they will never move. 'We are not going to go. We will stay here and die here. We will die for the land Gugama (the creator) gave us. We want to stay together on the same land as our grandparents because we were given this land by God.'

Survival International

The Charente

The area known as
'Cognac and Charente'
lies inland of the west
coast of France, the river
Charente itself reaching
the sea just south of
La Rochelle.

The mature river here
winds lazily and secretly
amongst the lush
undulating agricultural land
where vines, sunflowers and
cereals grow in abundance.

Villages are small
and the people appear
to be very much 'of the land'.
Roads are quiet, often almost
traffic free for hours,
and edged by numerous species of
wild flowers and butterflies.

It is indeed a very peaceful place,
threaded through by the great river
working its way to the sea,
watering the fertile land on its
way, and ignoring entirely
the small doings of
both man and beast
whose life blood it is.

There are towns, of course –
Cognac and Jarnac, for
example, with ancient
traditions and distilleries.
They grew up around the
river, and the river has sustained
their people and industries
for countless years.

Peace and tranquillity were the
main impressions, and a feeling that
the great river had a deep silent
heartbeat all of its own, imbuing
the area with a wonderful
sense of scale.

Margot Arthurton
England

Creative Carelessness

They cannot take away your sky, Lord,
Though they try –
With their toxic gas emission
And their CFC pollutions
And their smog-creating clouds.
It's still there.
Blue and black
In day and night-time.
Sun and moon and stars that glisten,
Clouds that glow and glower and rumble.
Sunset flare and sunrise glory
Ever changing
Yet eternal.
Yours, Lord.
How dare we ignore it
As if nothing we could do will permanently harm it?

Make us aware of our responsibilities.

They cannot take away your earth, Lord,
Or its worth.
With their underground nuclear testing
And their careless deforestation
And their war-torn mass destruction.
It's still there.
Rainbow coloured
Plants and animals,
Trees and fruit and birds and fishes,
Grass and grain and sparkling water,
Land and sea and soaring mountain –
Your provisions
For your children.
Yours, Lord.
How dare we misuse it
As if we need do nothing to protect it?

Make us aware of our stewardship.

Please, Lord,
Before it's too late.

Marjorie Dobson
England

A Monotheistic Reflection on Pagan Cycles of the Year

From atoms to planets eternity changes;
the hues and the colours that cover the earth,
through seasons and cycles, the world rearranges,
but sure is the love that has brought us to birth.

The wind and the weather distort vegetation,
the breakers are pounding and shaping the shore.
Our lives are spun round as each grief re-determines
the things that are doubtful and those that are sure.

Amid all this turmoil, this change and mutation,
the metamorphosis of living and strife,
one thing remains constant, relentless, determined:
that God goes on loving in death as through life.

Andrew Pratt
England

Creation in Travail

One of the most evocative passages in the New Testament is St Paul's description of creation in travail in Romans, chapter 8. The apostle uses childbirth as a metaphor for what is going on in creation, in human beings and in the outworking of God's purposes on earth. It is a great longing in which hope contends with apprehension and anticipation with fear. Science and technology perform great things, but greed, violence and evil misuse them and threaten life. The 'bondage to decay' which is threatening the birth of the new order could mean the forces of reaction that fear the changes that must be made. Or it could mean an introverted attitude that can think of nothing else but personal security and well being and how it is going to be affected. Christians are not exempt from the uncertainties at the heart of life; it is a sign of their solidarity with the rest of society. They cannot join the cynical game of decrying politicians, social planners and do-gooders. They dare not mock the failure of the liberal dream. They are involved. But they do have God's Spirit and the assurance of deliverance. Thus they pray and work for the birth of the new order.

R J McKelvey
England

Celebrating the Uniqueness of Trees

Nothing of our coconut tree is ever lost, Its fibrous trunk is used for lumber. Its leaves are used for roofing of nipa houses, while the midribs of its leaves are made into broomsticks. Its fruits are delightful nourishment and its fresh juice, besides satisfying thirst has a healing value for kidney ailments. Both fruit and juice are used in a variety of Filipino dishes. When only the husk remains even this is made useful in cleaning of wooden floors. The decorative arts find good material in its dry husk and leaves.

Coconut planters have their workers take great risks to climb high and gather the oil which is used in cooking as well as for wine-making and healthy hair.

Coconut groves beautify our seashores for they rise tall and strong. They too, weather any storm.

Let us celebrate the stately beauty and usefulness of our Coconut tree.

Response: **Spirit of the Coconut tree**
Let us be one with you!

The young leaves and fruits of the Tamarind tree are used for souring certain Filipino dishes – the 'sinigang'. The ripe pods are eaten or made into syrups, beverages and candied sweets.

Let us celebrate these gifts of our Tamarind tree.

Response: **Spirit of the Tamarind tree,**
Let us be one with you!

The Malunggay tree has tiny green leaves often used in Filipino dishes like 'tinolang manok'. Herbalists say it is very rich in iron, and its seeds when dried may be eaten raw and can be used as a diuretic. The poultice of the leaves is used for laxative purposes and for glandular swellings.

Let us celebrate the rich, medicinal properties of the Malunggay tree.

Response: **Spirit of the Malunggay tree**
Let us be one with you!

The Avocado seed can easily sprout and grow into a tree whose leaves are plucked for avocado tea. Its pear-shaped fruit is either green or violet brown. A single ripe fruit is commonly equated in nutritious value as equivalent to six eggs. It used to be a common, ordinary fruit until its nourishing richness became known and appreciated.

Let us celebrate our friend, the Avocado tree

Response: **Spirit of the Avocado tree**
              Let us be one with you!

The Mango tree is a rich source of vitamin C. It produces luscious green fruits which turn yellow when ripe. Its leaves when boiled in water can bring cure for colds or when dipped in hot water and applied externally can ease arthritic pains.
The oil of the seed is useful in chronic malarial fever. Mango leaves are found in the famous 'pito-pito' herbal tea. (pito = seven leaves of tea)

Let us celebrate the rich medicinal properties of the Mango tree.

Response: **Spirit of the Mango tree**
              Let us be one with you!

The Narra, which is our Filipino national tree is known for its hardness, usefulness and rapid growth as well as for its adaptability to any kind of soil. It is a windfirm tree that can withstand strong storms. Its branches spread wide like a gigantic umbrella and provide shade and shelter to many creatures.

May these sturdy trees be a symbol of our steadfastness in faith and hope in Christ. May we constantly anchor our life in Christ who is our all.

Pax Christi
The Philippines

The Rainforest

If we enter a rainforest and allow our energies to merge with the energies that we find there then the rainforest may be a place where our roots are able to penetrate through the soft soil into the reality of our billions of years of carbon journey through the universe. Various truths which heretofore had been merely 'scientific' become authentic, personal and yes, spiritual. We may now penetrate to a truly deep ecology.

Much of the apathy and paralysis that prevents us from throwing our lives into Earth-defence and Earth-healing is a product of our shrunken sense of self. As long as we remain identified with the social fictions we have been conditioned to believe compose our 'self', it is indeed difficult to find the energy and resolve necessary for the successful defence of Nature. If we can allow our sense of self to deepen, however, then our actions can be seen to be 'self-defence', for the Nature that we defend is no other than our own.

Once we have experienced the fierce joy of life that attends extending our identity into 'external' Nature, boundless energy and enthusiasm are ours for the asking. Once we realise that the Nature in here and the Nature out there are one and the same, then we act with passion and wisdom to prevent the destruction of the Tree of Life on which we humans are but a tiny blossom.

John Seed
Australia

Rosy Periwinkle
(Catharanthus Roseus)

This rainforest plant has provided a drug, effective in fighting leukaemia, one of the most intractable of cancers.

It is now grown commercially in several countries but Madagascar from which it first came has received little, if anything, for its contribution to human well being. The remaining rainforests and wild life are under much pressure as the population increases. Madagascar is one of the world's poorest countries, therefore, it would seem just that the country should be valued for this contribution to medicine.

Source Unknown

Rainsong

It falls in a veil,
The evening rain …
Like wafting gauze,
Diffusing all peripheries
Between the seer
And the seen;
It gentles free the clinging dust,
And coaxes into green
The faded grass –
Upon whose glistening spears
It hangs and gleams
Like jewels upon a skein …
Soft fall, and welcome
Mantle – over all embraced
In misting drift –
To blend the vespered edge
Of brief dark's swift
Encroach, and crystallise
Through vapour furled
The cool uncurling
Of the coming night.
So may the hours
Restore the thirsty earth
With distillation sweet …
Until the early light
Rejects in tatters grey
Retreating clouds,
And pinks the fresh perfection
Of the infant day
In opal shrouds of gossamer.

Margot Arthurton
England

Drought

Small wind quipples,
Ripples in the cup –
Stippling the cobbles,
Slipping just a sip,
A tantalising taste …
Settling the dust
On the drought-dry crust
Of the summer's heat …

Dry leaf skitters,
Scuttles in the gutter –
Unsettled, brittle …
Catching at random
In the dirt-dry drain …

Old sky mutters,
Echoes from afar …
Sun shafts out –
Laughs at the draught,
Puts the rain to rout,
Mocking at the storm –
Perpetuating drought …

Dessicating sunshine
Blazing on and on …

Old man sighs –
For his harvest is gone …

Margot Arthurton
England

A Prayer of Repentance

God of drowning coral atoll,
      Pacific-swamped,
            we are sorry.
God of burning rainforest,
      devoured by greed,
            we are sorry.
God of lost species,
      creation crucified,
            we are sorry.
God of punctured atmosphere,
      ozone-depleted,
            we are sorry.
God of vanished hedgerows,
      that got in our way,
            we are sorry.

God of forgiveness,
      abused yet eternal,
            we are glad.
God of hope,
      believing we can change,
            we are glad.
God of life,
      fragile and fun,
            we are glad.
God of love,
      daringly humble,
            we are glad.
God of peace,
      world-embracing,
            we are glad.
God of Jesus,
      Kingdom-bringing,
            we are glad.

God of all the world,
      with you our sadness is real for the sins of humanity.
But with you our sadness blossoms into gladness,
      through the confirming power of your Spirit
          and in the redeeming name of your Son.
Amen.

Neil Thorogood
England

Fragility and Strength

I loved the little islands, the many islands,
we call Polynesia.
They were exposed to the great ocean's power
but guarded by their coral reefs.
On the coral the storm swell broke
in clouds of spray, drifting across the shallows.
They looked so fragile, mere whisps of land,
ready to be blown away;
but here for a thousand years
people have made a home
and formed a culture with dignity, humour and hope.

> Just another ton of CO
> another thousand cars
> a dozen new power stations,
> let's build our towers to touch the sky.

So the islanders wait for the high tide
on the next full moon,
and wonder what will save them now.

Help us, Universal God, to act as
sisters and brothers in the one human family.

Bernard Thorogood
Australia

Prayers from Cumbria
(an area of north-west England)

From the stench of organo phosphates
on summer evenings
O God deliver us

From spinners spreading pesticides
on flowerless green deserts
where no bird sings
O God deliver us

From spraypacks delivering death
to meadow thistles and butterflies
O God deliver us

From the grubbing out of dry stone walls
and ancient hedgerow habitats
O God deliver us

From nuclear fallout
and contamination
O God deliver us

From miscarriage,
low sperm counts,
deformity and illness
O God deliver us

From diseased fish
and poisoned shellfish
O God deliver us

From polluted water
and frogless ponds
O God deliver us

From belching smoke
in streets of old grey towns
O God deliver us

From asthma and bronchitis
O God deliver us

From tragedy and sudden death on our roads
O God deliver us

From pesticides in our food
O God deliver us

For pigs reeking in intensive squalor
O God deliver us

For battery hens
confined in featherless servitude
O God deliver us

For milk cows
bred into obscene deformity
O God deliver us

For flowerless, treeless,
overgrazed lands
O God deliver us

For breeding birds and mammals
destroyed by silage machinery
O God deliver us

For lonely old people
with no bus service
    We pray

For suicidal farmers
with no security
    We pray

For agricultural workers
with damaged lungs and weakened bodies,
grown prematurely old
    We pray

For children with leukaemia
and childhood cancers
    We pray

For marginalised, poisoned, diminishing wildlife
    We pray

O God, may we see in our time
pigs in coppiced woodlands,
cows in wildflower meadows,
curlew and skylarks in lowland pastures,
hens in orchards
and teeming fish in clean waters.

May we leave for our children
a safe, clean and free environment,
a world where health and beauty
count for more than financial gain.

Marlene Phillips
England

Lord of the Wind

Dear Lord of the wind, let your Word fly free
spreading love from here to eternity,
encompassing all, encompassing all.

East wind, harsh wind,
screaming off the marsh wind,
scouring empty parks leaving ice-bare bough;
chimneys moan and shudder
and ice-bound engines judder
while late blooms droop and blacken, frost purifies the plough.
Dear Lord of the wind, let your Truth fly free
spreading love from here to eternity,
encompassing all, encompassing all.

North wind, snow wind,
tingling Eskimo wind,
drifting silently as each crevice fills;
cleansing grimy alleys
transforming ravaged valleys
as crystals cling to rubbish and early daffodils.
Dear Lord of the wind, let your Grace fly free
Spreading love from here to eternity,
Encompassing all, encompassing all.

South wind, soft wind,
scarcely keep aloft wind,
bumbling off the beach past sunshaded prams;
pollen laden breezes
commingle as it eases
by factory and car park and fields of full-grown lambs.
Dear Lord of the wind, let your Peace fly free
spreading love from here to eternity,
encompassing all, encompassing all.

West wind, salt wind,
tempestuous to a fault wind,
surging from the deep over ripened land;
sheaves are stooked with apples
as churches, schools and chapels
rejoice at harvest riches and bless God's bounteous hand.
Dear Lord of the wind, let our joy fly free
spreading love from here to eternity,
encompassing all, encompassing all.

Toni Allfrey
England

Callum's Different Holiday

We've just been to Thailand for a month. (We've camped and climbed in Wales and cycled in Holland but never been on such a big adventure)! Next time I'll be in senior school so I won't get time off. We took our workbooks along. Mum used to live in Thailand – her Dad worked there. It was a long flight but we liked the food. First we stayed at the coast. It was quiet. We swam a lot and went out in boats. The fishermen were friendly. We visited another beach place – it was noisy and boring. Later from Bangkok, we went to the Bridge on the River Kwai and found a cottage to stay in. My Dad said he really liked that train trip. We found a man with a minibus who took us places we wanted for a price we fixed; he could take his wife and child along too, which was nice for them.

In Chiang Mai we stayed in the Christian Guest House and met nice people. A Korean pastor with three boys said that four of us must be a lot of work! The museums were really good; temples weren't really our thing. After that we flew to near Laos. Young people who grew up in a Thai Children's Home our family knows have a project in the hills there. We got to stay in a missionary's house who was away; so we weren't a trouble. We ate great food and went places with the team of young people. The men had motor bikes and gave us rides. It was really cool. The leader had a degree from the top university and used to have a great job; but he left. He heard God's call to help the hill people. There are lots of tribes around, Hmong, Akha, Karen etc. All in different villages. We went with the team up the loopy hills and usually spent hours in the villages. The houses are wooden on stilts. The ground floor is upstairs and made of split bamboo. We played with the kids and learned some words and games. I think the men talked about farming and the women about crafts. They weave on looms like boxes and do embroidery. The team people don't tell villagers what to do; they ask what they need and make plans together. They'll help but don't give money. My Dad says that's the best way – to encourage them to support themselves. Back in town we visited workplaces. The silver-makers' place was best with about forty men working. They had a football field and knew more about UK teams than we did! My Mum specially liked the hill villages. She said it reminded her of hill climbs in Nepal when she was fourteen. Poor children from tiny villages came to greet them, carrying such weak, sick babies. Since then, she always wanted to see families in far-away mountain villages getting proper help. We found a bible verse for what they need: 'The work they do will be successful and their children will not meet with disaster'. (Isaiah 65:23)

Grace Westerduin
with Callum Broadley, aged eleven
England

A Beautiful Carved Ball

Once there was a father who by profession was a carpenter. One day he called his children together and gave them a beautiful carved ball. He said to them, 'I'm giving this to you now so that you can look after it for me. Take care of it because I love this ball very much. I hope that you will learn to love it too, and will learn many things by learning to look after it.'

The children played with the ball and explored the carvings on its surface. One day they discovered that it opened up and inside were many more small intricately carved things.

Over the following years the ball was handed down from generation to generation. People forgot it had been a very special thing and it was taken outside and played with in the dirt. It was floated on puddles and thrown into trees. Bits got knocked off and dirt was ingrained in the carvings. No-one remembered how many little toys had been inside when it was new so no one bothered to check none had been lost. Besides it had got jammed together and would no longer open.

One day one of the great-great-great grandchildren of its maker decided to try to clean it up, but the glue wouldn't stick the unusual wood together, and the cleaning materials he used changed the colour and it began to look patchy.

'I wish I knew what it looked like in the beginning,' he said. 'I don't even know what the person who carved it looked like. I wish I had known him. I think I'd have liked to watch him at work. I could have learned a lot from him.'

He called all the family together. It took weeks to persuade them all to come. At this family meeting he said, 'We have had this ball in our family for generations. Once it must have been beautiful and just look at it now. We have neglected our duty as a family to care for this treasure. When we pass it on to our children I want it to look better than this.'

Different relations came up with different ideas. One searched all the family archives to see if there was any description of the ball when it was new. One researched into new and innovative methods of cleaning and repairing rare wooden objects. One meditated on how it might once have looked and tried to draw and paint these images.

It was one small child who took the ball lovingly in her hands. She sang to it while she stroked it and kissed it and felt all the ridges and bumps. Over the days and weeks whilst the adults were discussing and planning and writing letters and making phone calls, this child's love slowly brought the ball back to life. The intricate patterns began to emerge and once again it was possible to open it up. There were still quite a few little carvings inside, so the child loved them into freshness too. She counted them each day and if one went astray she searched it out and returned it carefully to its proper place.

Our world is like that ball. All the talking and planning in the world will not help to bring it back to the beautiful place it was when our Creator God entrusted it to our care. We can clean it up a bit with technology but we can only restore it with love.

Liz Gentil
England

Needed - Creative Thinking!

Palai * conveys a sense of desolation and separation;
degraded and which is no longer usable. Drought,
untended land and destruction by war and fire,
degraded land 2000 years ago in Tamil Nadu.

Today, the natural resources of Tamil Nadu are under
severe threat. The forests and with them our bio-diversity
are diminishing. The fresh water sources are less and are
continually being polluted. Ocean pollution is reducing
the fish population and sullying our beaches and water.

Mushrooming urban populations place great stress on the
services of water, drainage, sewage treatment and garbage
disposal. Industrial pollution contaminates air, water and
land. Our ever expanding population places tremendous
and expanding demands on our natural resources.

Creative thinking and application are needed to solve these
problems. Responsible, caring citizens must be alert to the
misuse of services by themselves and by the officials they
elect. The good people of Tamil Nadu are called forth.

Palai is degraded or polluted land
This writing was seen at an ecological/environmental exhibition

Dakshina Chitra
Chennai, Tamil Nadu, south India

El Nino

The west coast of South America is normally one of the driest places on earth. But
every three or four years the weather pattern changes. The sea warms up, fish
disappear and freak storms cause mudslides that can wash houses away. This
weather disturbance called El Nino is part of a natural cycle.

The polar regions are the last true wilderness left on earth but change is taking
place there. Pipelines carry oil and gas across the Arctic tundra and more and more
passenger ships visit Antarctica's shores. Global warming is melting the polar ice
disrupting the lives of penguins along with other birds and animals.

Source Unknown

A Prayer for Sensitive Travellers

Lord of all nations but one world,
help me to be sensitive to other people's cultures and traditions.
When I am far from home, enable me to tread lightly upon the soil and
with you beside me, travel safely until my homecoming.
May I be willing to find friendship in the company of fellow travellers and
always greet strangers at my door.
In your name's sake.
Amen

Kevin Fray
England

Precaution

You know why
he turned both of them out
don't you?
Well, Adam would only
have started up
a logging company
in the primordial forest,
felling the Tree of Life
for mahogany toilet seats.

And Eve?
She would have taken over
the virgin beauty
of the shore-line,
promoted herself
to Managing Director
of Paradise Holidays Incorporated.

And then if not before
God would have been
turned out of Eden.

Cecily Taylor
England

Tide Turning

The wave moves inwards, swelling, breaking, pounding, surging
Frothy white topping translucent greens
Power and majesty dispersing to ripples and sparkle
Creation's first day

The wave moves inwards, gathering, calling, wetting, bracing
Invigorating deep to shallow
Splashing and swimming ringing with laughter and fun
Recreation and play

The wave moves inwards, threatening, turbid, viscous, smelling
Black-topped murky opaque grey
Oil and detergent smothering dead fish and birds
Desecration, dismay

The wave moves inwards, cleansing, refreshing, pulverising, redeeming
Dispersing sin, reviving hope
Nature with nurture, stewardship of life
Re-creation God's way.

David Pickering
England

A Paradise of Monsters

In the beginning was the World Bank;
the helicopters of the World Bank,
Fiji Development Bank
and the Fiji Ministry of Tourism,
hovered over the mangrove sandy Denarau Island.
They saw that it was formless
and they dreamed of Paradise.
A Tourist Resort Master Plan was made.

In the first stage they created a bridge;
from Nadi, rocks and soil were bulldozed across,
coconut palms and trees uprooted and replanted on the island.
In the second, third, fourth and fifth stages
an eighteen hole golf course, tennis court, beaches,
a jetty and boating harbour were created.
And they looked and whispered, 'Well done.'

In the sixth stage the World Bank, the IMF and the Fiji Development Bank said,
'Let us make one in our own image.'
Then the first monster was created
which was named 'The Regent'
'Let us make a Helper for the Regent.'
Then the second monster was created and named
'The Sheraton'.
They looked and said, 'Multiply and fill the Ocean'.

Written after participants to A Workshop on Tourism held in Nadi,
Fiji had visited the reclaimed Denarau Island, south Pacific

Dick Avi
Papua New Guinea

I Dreamed of A Perfect World

Did I dare to dream?
Did I dream last night?

I cannot remember.

Did I dream?

How could I forget!

I dreamed of a perfect world!
Of food enough for all,
Of clean water for all,
Of homes with light and space,
Made of materials to last.

Medical and dental care,
Nor more pain,
No more wars!

How could I forget!
My dream.

When I was a little girl
I woke up before my dream
was complete.

Older and wiser now but
my dream is still not complete.
Maybe I will try again tonight,
to dare to dream
and remember!

Barbara Oakes
England

The bird that wants to survive

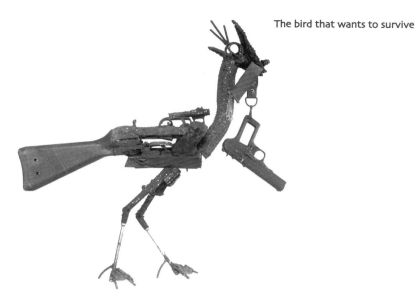

From Swords into Ploughshares
Transforming Arms into Art

(An exhibition from Mozambique at the OXO Centre, London, UK)

'I tell people that sleeping with a gun in your hand is like sleeping with a snake – one day it will turn round and bite you. We tell people we are not disarming you. We are transforming your guns into ploughshares, so you can cultivate your land and get your daily bread.'

Dom Dinis Sengulane
Bishop of Lebombo, Mozambique

Other quotes and captions beside the art exhibits

Calm after the storm. After mass destruction the first sign of movement is usually the stirring of insects.

In war everything is destroyed – human lives, birds, animals, the infrastructure of a country.

Savouring peace
The ends of peace are very important.
The creation of a flower, a flute, a whistle ...
We need to bring in allegro (lightness) to savour peace.

Transforming Arms into Art
Christian Aid

A Positive Husband

Ramalingappa is always smiling and optimistic. He is respected in his village, in Tumkur District, south-western Karnataka, south India and in the Public Works Department, where he monitors the progress of road construction.

Aged thirty-eight he and his wife Mallakka, aged thirty, have three girls and a boy, aged from two to thirteen years. Their first male child died at the age of five months, due to severe fever and diarrhoea. Mallakka became very depressed which caused impaired mental health. The prescribed medication made her worse and caused incontinence. Chronic anaemia resulted in a loss of energy.

Ramalingappa became responsible for caring for the family, including cooking, whilst continuing with his full time work. He became embarrassed at having to cope with a woman's work so he shut himself in the house to avoid criticism by the neighbours. Eventually he persuaded Mallakka to stop the medication. He encouraged her with an improved diet of fresh, green vegetables and very tasty curries. Non-vegetarian food was prepared to ensure that Mallakka had sufficient protein in her diet. Her health improved.

Eventually, Mallakka began to cook again and this made her feel good about herself. She gained in confidence and well-being. Ramalingappa used to tell her she was very healthy. He gained peace and encouragement from the fact that he was helping his wife.

Mallakka became pregnant and they had another daughter. Ramalingappa saw a great improvement in her health and he continued to encourage his wife as she took care of their daughter. The time came to give the child a naming ceremony. However, the stigma of mental illness meant that relations and neighbours would not visit the family. They spoke with his brother's family, explained the improved situation and invited them to attend the naming ceremony. His sister-in-law, who had not visited the village home whilst Mallakka was seriously ill, attended with other family members which pleased everyone.

Ramalingappa is well respected because of his experience and positive outlook. He is asked for advice by other carers who have family members suffering from mental illness.

When asked why he wants to help others, Ramalingappa replies 'My wife is suffering from a mental health problem. I am a human being and because my wife has this problem, helping others is my life.'

Geoffrey Duncan
England

A Benefit for the Earth

Envisat is a satellite which will observe our planet from eight kilometres above it. It will last for at least five years and will monitor environmentally crucial processes of our earth, as diverse as changes in ocean circulation, the ice caps, land use and atmospheric pollution. Envisat can observe slowly changing environmental phenomenon. It will detect where plants are threatened by drought as frequencies will be different from healthy plants with plenty of water.

Pamela Pavitt
England

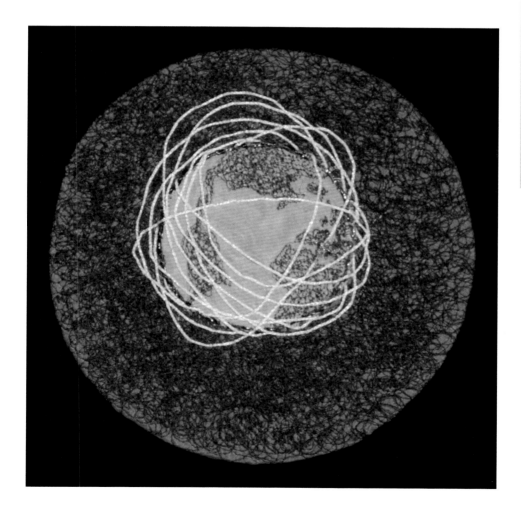

Towards Pleasant Lands

Arrange for one-third of the church to be decorated with fruit, vegetables, flowers, leaves, twigs, indoor plants, window boxes, flower tubs and other relevant items which focus on the local environment e.g. coastal flora and fauna, town gardens, park, city farms, with symbols or pictures of local architecture. Two-thirds should focus on vandalised or desecrated land and buildings, pictures or models of destroyed rain forests, drought prone areas, people driven off their land by multi-national greed, endangered species, poisoned land due to acid rain, various forms of pollution.

Call to Worship:

Leader: Every garden carefully tended,
Every flower lovingly arranged,
Every colour to be seen,
Every skill involved in the craft
Of every model and symbol displayed,
Every sea-shell, every stone, every green leaf

All: **Is a rainbow reflection of God's love.**

Bible Reflection:
When the rainbow appears in the clouds I will see it and remember the everlasting covenant between me and all living beings on earth (Genesis 9:16).

Hymn:

Invocatory Prayers:

Living Lord, we thank you for this new day
with all the promise of new life;
for the care and love which nurtures
beauty through nature which we see around us;
for beauty through buildings
for the creative skills of the artist, modeller, musician and writer
Praise be to God!

Multi-coloured Glory

Gracious God,
in the bright multi-coloured glory of Creation,
and the heartbeat rhythm of the seasons,
in the light of Christ we live,
our days and ways illuminated by your Spirit.
We bring our darknesses and our brightnesses –
all the shades and colours of our lives –
our winter, spring, summer, autumn
before you now in worship:
and we pray that as we seek to draw near to you,
we will know you near us and with us as we go.
In Jesus' name we pray:
Amen

Stephen Brown
England

The Lord's Prayer

Time with the Family:
To be planned beforehand – teachers and children should be asked to talk about what they like best about the place in which they live. Ask the children and adults to bring an item to church for this occasion.

At worship:
Display the brought items in addition to those already arranged. Ask people to talk about what pleases them best about their environment. Talk about the pleasures. Talk about the disappointments. What is necessary to provide the items which have been brought? Develop the fact that people need to use their creative skills to make the environment a pleasant place.

To Sing: Think of a world without any flowers
                  For the beauty of the earth
                  For the fruits of His creation

Ikebana

Ikebana is the ancient Japanese art of flower arranging. Traditionally flowers are placed at the altar of a shrine or temple or at a special place in the home known as the *tokonoma*. The creative skills of the family produce, through the flowers, a spirit of harmony which reflects the nature of the world. *Ikebana* is a way of developing a person's attitude and place in the world. Although this art form belongs to the Shinto religion there are Christians who use it to express their faith. The 'way of the flower' is considered as a means of worshipping God as creator and protector of the universe. Several strands of Christian belief make *ikebana* acceptable:
● belief in God as creator of all things and;
● humankind's responsibility for them (Genesis 1:26);

- a view that God teaches people about himself through creation
  (Matthew 6: 28 – 30);
- a reminder of God's continuing love in times of change (1 Peter 1:24 – 25).

Christian *ikebana* has incorporated these themes when dealing with human joy, in caring for others, suffering and the promise of new life.

Geoffrey Duncan
England

Bible Readings:
Genesis 9: 8 – 17
Matthew 6: 24 – 30
Psalm 104 (selected verses)

Earth Credo

Leader: I believe in the sacredness of the earth,
the integrity of the whole creation
and dignity of all people and creatures.

I believe in a gracious God who created humankind,
male and female in God's image
and gave them the gift and responsibility
to take care of the earth.

All: **We need to care.**

Leader: I believe we human beings have failed God and ourselves.
In the name of greed and 'development'
we have dominated the earth, degraded people and
creatures,
destroyed the forests, polluted the air, rivers and seas,
and have sacrificed the future of our children.

All: **We need to repent.**

Leader: I believe that when we destroy the earth we kill ourselves.
We need to preserve and protect the earth,
not only for our own survival,
but for the sake of Mother Earth.

All: **The time to change is now.**

Leader: I believe we need to change our ways, values,
lifestyles and ways of relating with creation.
Repent, fast and pray. Consume less ... waste not.
Work for justice and peace.
We should not covet our neighbour's timber,
butterflies, white sand beaches,

nearly extinct animals nor cheap labour.
We should not oppress children, indigenous people, women,
the homeless, refugees and victims of war.

All: **We need to live in defence of people and creation.**

Leader: For I believe in the interwovenness of life:
Creator and creatures ... Breath and prayer
Cosmic and individual ... Food and freedom
West, North, East, South ... Sexuality and spirituality ...
Ecology and theology.

I therefore commit myself,
together with other concerned people everywhere,
to take care of Mother Earth.
To advocate for peace and justice.
To choose and celebrate Life!

All: **These things I believe.**
Amen

Elizabeth Tapia
Philippines

Reflections/Sermon

Consider the global situation (locally and internationally) where the
environment is not a pleasant land;

- your local community;
- national situations;
- internationally – focus on one particular concern
  e.g. the destruction of rain forests;
- land used for buildings which destroy ways of life for rural farmers;
- the greed of globalisation and multinational corporations;
- the plight of indigenous peoples;
- fast disappearing Pacific Ocean islands due to global warming;
- the arms trade and war-torn countries

Hymn:

The Land is Holy

The land is from God and we are his people;
the land sustains us so we should sustain the land.
Why do we desecrate the land?
Why do we pump impurities into the air?
Why do we fill the rivers with filth?
Since the earth is the Lord's let us respect it.

Since the land is holy, let us revere it.
Since the world is God's creation, let us honour him
in our enjoyment of the land and all its produce.
God gave us Eden; we made hell on earth.
Now let us return to the Lord and obey his word;
then we shall inherit Eden once more.

Responsive Prayer

Leader: Loving Creator,
               you care for the land by sending rain;
               you make it fertile and fruitful.
               What a rich harvest you provide.

Response: **All your creation sings for joy.**

Leader: When we take care of the land,
               sowing seed and reaping harvest.

Response: **All your creation sings for joy.**

Leader: When we keep streams and rivers clean,
               when we respect the purity of the lakes and seas.

Response: **All your creation sings for joy.**

Leader: When we refuse to hunt down animals,
               when we take care of them and value their work.

Response: **All your creation sings for joy.**

Leader: When we recognise that we are one family,
               brothers and sisters together, connected to the land.

Response: **All your creation sings for joy
               for you bless us abundantly all our days.**

Leader: I cannot be an enemy to the land
               for the land gives me life.
               I cannot buy or sell the land
               for it is a free gift of God to the people.
               People and land are one creation
               and when their essential unity is broken
               the land and the people suffer.
               All creation cries in pain
               until the redeemer buys its peace again.

John Johansen-Berg
England

Hymn:

Blessing:

May the Blessing of the Earth, Our Mother

> May the blessing of the earth, our mother,
> nourish and sustain you.
>
> May the blessing of the sky, our sister,
> lift up your tired heart.
>
> May the blessing of the sun, our brother,
> smile his warmth upon you.
>
> May the voices that call in the wind
> and thunder in the raging sea,
> bless you with their strength.
>
> May the flames that dance in the fire
> and burn in life's longings for love
> bless you with their power.
>
> May the blessings of earth, sky, fire, wind and water,
> Grant you peace and joy as creation's son or daughter.

Jean Mortimer
England

Notes:

Arrange a Church and Community visit to a local garden, park, city farm or local beauty spot.
Look at places in inner cities that have been developed as areas of beauty.
Establish a link rural/urban and discover your different environments.

Geoffrey Duncan
England

To Earn Our Rice and Bread

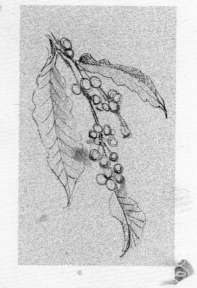

Sower and Reaper Rejoice Together

Sower and reaper rejoice together
For the harvest is good

Sower and reaper rejoice together
For the rains came, and the sun shone

Sower and reaper rejoice together
There is food and water for all

Living God, your Spirit hovered over the water
And you created the good things of the earth for all to share.
You are the God of hope, whose Spirit is power and love.
Be with us as we build and plant for a future
Where all your people share in the harvest
And no one goes hungry

Let sower and reaper rejoice together
For the harvest is good

Sower and reaper rejoice together
There is food and water for all.

Linda Jones
England

Fruits of Earth

The fruits of earth are meant for all,
for all are children who depend
upon the need for food and clothes,
we sense the purpose you intend;
so may we pay what's just and fair
for other's work –
this is our prayer.

Cecily Taylor
England

Self Worth

After a life of struggle the chance to get involved in Fairtrade has
brought a new dimension to my life. There is a great feeling of self
worth that comes out of being involved in this work.

Sourubarani, a tea picker
Sri Lanka

Shakuhachi
(Bamboo Flute)

The *shakuhachi* is certainly Japan's most well-known woodwind instrument.
A vertically held bamboo flute, it is made from the very bottom of a bamboo
tree. Bamboo is hollow except for nodes, which are spaced at intervals along
the pipe. They are knocked out to form the complete hollow length of the
pipe. Four finger holes are put on the front of the instrument and a
thumbhole on the back. The mouthpiece is the open top of the pipe itself
with the front side cut at a slight angle to facilitate blowing the instrument.

Although the placement of holes and tuning of the instrument is a very
delicate process, the instrument is of a basically simple construction. It is this
fact, however, which allows for very complex techniques in playing the
instrument such as the use of the breath with changes in the blowing angle
for great or minute changes in sound quality, or partial-holding of finger
holes to make delicate pitch changes.

The instrument takes its name from its standard length of one foot (*shaku*)
and eight (*hachi*) parts of a foot (called *sun*), approximately 54 centimetres.
There are other lengths of the instrument as well, all with the general name
of *shakuhachi*.

Anil Kumar Patil
south India

A Donkey Plough?

A plough may not be hi-tech but to a hungry family in Sudan it's a masterpiece of 'cutting edge' technology. It is simple. It is cheap. It can help a hungry family feed themselves – not just for a day but for years to come.

People in Darfur, Sudan thought they had tried everything. The soil was heavy, the climate unforgiving. Too poor to afford camels for ploughing they worked the land the hard way … by hand. They could only watch as their crops failed and their children suffered.

Thanks to the hard work of local people and the know-how of Intermediate Technology Development Group (ITDG) staff, ploughs are helping families to grow all the food they need, permanently.

Scrap-heap or cutting edge?

First, the plough.
Working with local farmers, staff of ITDG built one out of scrap metal with a blade perfectly suited to local conditions. The blade turns furrows that can hold on to precious rainwater for weeks.

The blade turns furrows that can hold on to precious rainwater for weeks

Pack animal or powerhouse?

Next, the donkey. Villagers laughed when the ITDG team first suggested using a donkey. But they had seen it work and they proved it works in Darfur. With a donkey pulling the plough, yields can rise by up to 500%.

With a donkey pulling the plough, crop yields can rise by up to 500%

Rags or riches?
A plough, a donkey and to join them up a soft harness was devised stuffed with just straw, cotton and rags which any family could make for themselves.

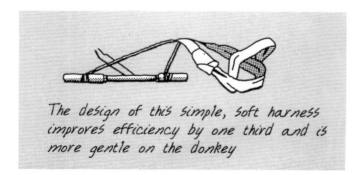

The design of this simple, soft harness improves efficiency by one third and is more gentle on the donkey

Intermediate Technology Development Group
England

Heading for the Beach

I remember thinking she must be hot,
the paving a rough seat, her tattered
umbrella offering poor shade
from the African sun.

We parked our air-conditioned car
right by her, began unloading
mats, parasols, picnics, factor 35
to protect our fair faces.

Dazzled by the Durban sun,
I thought she sat in a sea
of rubbish, paper fluttering
round her feet like restless birds

until the razor blade flashed silver
and cut through plastic carriers,
leaving long ribbons flowing
down from her fingers.
Hours later, ice creams melting,
I watched the transformation,
plastic to yarn and looping stitches,
neat rows of crochet growing,

spotted the multi-coloured mats
displayed on the pavement,
the way her fingers and eyes
never connected, but her smile

sought out passers-by,
me included, and the way
I fumbled for coins to buy
the bags I usually binned

now transformed into something
useful, beautiful and strong,
the world's waste made new
by a woman's quick fingers.

Fiona Ritchie Walker
England

To Attain Their Noble Dreams

Salay Handmade Paper Industry Inc (SHAPII) is based in the Philippines and is a company committed to sustainable livelihoods for more than two hundred employees - mainly women. Its business objective is 'to make use of indigenous raw materials and turn these into novel, hand-crafted products to attain their big and noble dreams embodied in their mission'.

Their mission statement includes the following:

- to give a decent livelihood to our people;

- to help give identity to our town, Salay;

- to help in developing the Filipino by instilling the virtues of patriotism, honesty, loyalty, self-reliance, hard work, patience, love of God and discipline through the art of handmade papermaking and its related activities;

- to free our land from the waste grass, cogon, so that it may be utilised for the planting of better crops to improve the lives of our people;

- to develop international friendship through the art of handmade papermaking.

Natural ingredients used by Salay include fresh cogon grass, which is ox-drawn to town where it is cut, cooked and processed entirely by hand. Each piece of paper is created in a mould and deckle couched in cloth, pressed by hand and dried by air, sun or steam, for days.

Other raw materials used include pineapple leaves, locally grown flowers, leaves and weeds, plus waste silk cocoons which are transformed into beautiful flowers to decorate cards and notebooks.

Salay is just one of the groups that provides fair trade organisations like Traidcraft with a wide range of paper products using unusual, natural materials.

Salay/Traidcraft
Phillipines/England

From A Paper Maker

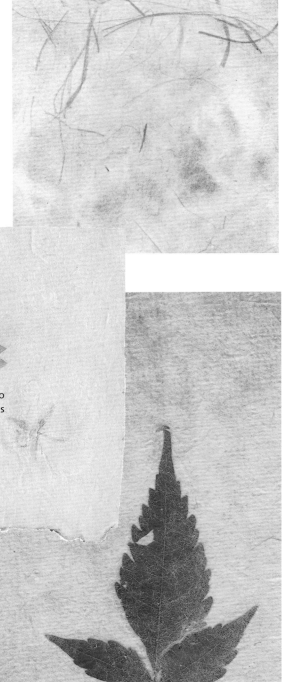

Colours, fibres
and flowers
texture, beauty
and forms.

They make my world go round.

When I make these sheets
my heart swells
with the fulfilment
of creation.

It is only paper
but it's also me!

And when I hand you this
to keep and enjoy.

A little of me is
with you.

A little of God's wonder
I give to you!

Loreta Capistrano
Phillipines

Paper from Mulberry Bark

It's being produced in Nan City, an elegant riverside settlement in north-east Thailand, between Chiang Mai and the Lao border.

In the nearby hill country, where the traditional life-style is under threat, tribal women earn a small income by selling the bark of mulberry trees – 'sa'. This bark, – happily a renewable source – is stripped from the trees by the women and baskets-full are sold for processing in the city.

In Nan, this small-scale industry employs about eight workers who clearly enjoy what they do. Ideally a share of the profits should be recycled towards hill tribe education as in several sponsored craft projects.

The work is carried out in sheds in a spacious green compound near the river. The mulberry bark is soaked in open baths of water for some days. It is stirred regularly. Gradually, the substance turns into a gluey pulp with a characteristic smell. When it has dried to the required consistency, more water is added and a rectangular frame with wire mesh is introduced into the tank. The pulp which adheres to this will form the sheet of paper. Eventually, the racks are lifted out and stacked on top of each other for drying.

The most striking aspect of this cottage industry becomes evident when pairs of these drying-racks are propped up against each other in tent-like formation. The compound looks like a farm of solar panels.

When the sheets of mulberry paper are slipped loose from the frames, ready for sale, the workers feel pride in their hand-crafted product. Other processes are carried out elsewhere. The coarse, tough material can be dyed and shaped into items such as photo-frames and albums, to hold, perhaps, tourists' memories of a culture briefly visited.

Grace Westerduin
England

God of the Workplace

Dear God of the workplace,
who is present in every transaction,
watching for the well-being of working people everywhere.
You know each person involved in producing, trading and consuming the products that
I buy and sell.
When I trade, I become entwined with every link in the trade chain.
Likewise, be entwined in me and through me
let your presence be revealed.
For your name's sake.
Amen

Kevin Fray
England

Thoughts over a Grapefruit Juice and a Sesame Bun

18.00 hours, after a day's work, in the crypt of St Martin's in the Fields, London on a beautiful, cool Autumn evening.

An interesting mix of people
        – all ages –
Plenty of lively conversation
An attractive vegetarian menu
Profits go toward the project
        for Homeless People.
Hungry people are fed
Distressed people are given shelter
– that's their Harvest –
being fed and given shelter.
God of the (w)holistic Church
God of many satisfied stomachs
We have come in from the real world
to draw breath
to engage in social chit-chat
to wait for family or friends
to have a pleasant evening
at the theatre
but then …
where are you God of Love
in the wars which tear the world apart?
Where are you Christ of Compassion
In the refugee situations
and the ever increasing numbers of devastated people?
Where are you Holy Spirit of Comfort
where there is no harvest for millions of people?
In the places where there is hunger
Drought … floods … poverty
Greed … ignorance … bigotry.

You are there,
God of Love,
Christ of Compassion,
Holy Spirit of Comfort
in the normal every day patterns of life,
and
I know that there are many people in the Faith Communities;
the humanitarian organisations;
the charities who are working round the clock to alleviate suffering
to take a Harvest to suffering people
and then

I give thanks.

People are striving for better days,
for the time when the hungry
and thirsty
shall have their needs met;
for peace and reconciliation,
and where that happens there you are
in the midst,
getting on with life.
Yes – God of Love,
I and many others will stick in there.
Amen

Geoffrey Duncan
England

Meditation on a Mange-tout Pea

What do you see in this small green vegetable?
A restaurant delicacy, all very nouvelle cuisine?
A famine infested pea steam rolled flat for weight-watchers?

Each pea tells a story:
grown from Zimbabwe to Guatemala,
but not eaten by the locals.
These cash-crops are air-freighted to European markets
in the name of 'economic restructuring'.

Not grown for flavour, just for looks.
Not grown for nutrition, just for cash.
Not grown for people, just for markets.
Not grown for food, just for debt.

And eaten by us:
struggling to stand by the poor,
trying to be generous to the needy,
aiming to share with our neighbours,
wanting to be open-handed.

Even the poor grow peas just for us.

Get ready to proclaim Jubilee!
Let debts be remitted,
that all God's people might live a sweet life,
like pods bursting with ripeness.

Janet Lees
England

Basmati Takeaway

Basmati – the 'crown jewel' of South Asian rice – commands a premium price in international markets. Approximately one million hectares in India and 0.75 million hectares in Pakistan are planted to basmati varieties. Cultivated by more than one million small farmers, the rice has been grown for centuries in the Himalayan region, with farmers selecting and maintaining the varieties.

In 1997 a Texas based company, RiceTec, won a patent (US 5,663,484) on novel basmati rice lines, seeds, grains, plants and their progeny. The patent included a total of 20 broad claims on a number of varieties.

The scope of the patent extended to varieties grown anywhere in the western hemisphere and farmers believed export markets to the US were threatened when RiceTec sold US-grown basmati rice in the US under the brandnames of Texmati and Kasmati.

The patent shocked South Asian farmers and it was condemned as 'biopiracy' by a world wide coalition of ninety civil society organisations , including the Canadian-based Rural Advancement Foundation International (RAFI), Action Aid and the Swiss–based Berne Declaration. A global campaign was launched; Action Aid ran an advertising campaign in British newspapers to publicise the issue. The Government of India challenged the patent. In August 2001 the US Patent and Trademark Office (USPTO) struck down fifteen out of the twenty original claims.

The USPTO said the rice lines, plants and grains that RiceTec claimed were basically identical to basmati rice grown in the Himalayan region of South Asia – there were records which described the characteristics as 'prior art' – and therefore could not be claimed as 'novel' and patented.

Five claims, however, on three specific varieties still stand. On hearing the ruling MPs stormed the floor of the India lower parliament and ministers from India and Pakistan met to plan their next steps.

Campaigners worldwide are urging the USPTO to strike off the last remaining claims and take measures to outlaw patents that pirate the knowledge and resources of farmers and indigenous people.

Action Aid
England

Give With Love

Give with love to those who hunger,
not just bread for this day's need,
but with plough and grain and water,
tools to help them always feed.
When God's people work together
life is planted with each tiny seed.

Give with hope to those who suffer,
ignorant and poorly fed.
Teach them how to grow and flourish,
give them power to earn their bread.
When God's people work together
rich and poor in fellowship can tread.

Give a life that is worth living
to the child without a home,
heal her future by your actions,
let her growing be your own.
When God's people work together
children laugh and play for hope is known.

Give with faith when there is darkness
and the answers are not clear.
Try to offer peace and justice,
speak so that the nations hear.
When God's people work together
love can always overcome the fear.

Give with joy and seek no profit,
life is meant for all to share,
life in all its rich abundance
is for people everywhere.
When God's people work together
God alive is also working there.

Colin Ferguson
England

Daily Rice or Maize Instead

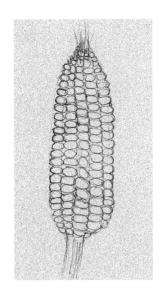

In Jesus' name we bless and break
this sacred gift of daily bread;
he shares with friends in other lands
their daily rice or maize instead.

Some prize a chalice; others clasp
a cup of china, wood or steel;
yet each in word and deed recalls
that Upper Room, that final meal.

He tells us here, 'Remember me –
not long ago and far away
but present at this table now,
your servant and your Lord today.'

We join his friends throughout the world
to bring our heartfelt gratitude;
And pray that hungry souls may find
In Christ himself their spirits' food.

Tune: Eisenach or Ely

Basil Bridge
England

Combine Harvester

Gone are the days of following the horse
in preparing the ground for sowing
and reaping the harvest of the fields.
Now is the day of motorised tractors
and the technology of the combine harvester.
Today if 'big' is not deemed beautiful
it is at least reckoned more effective.
The farmer now must have an eye to profit,
so his computer draws up programmes
enabling efficient management of spreading fields.

John Johansen-Berg
England

What a World

Heart of Heaven - Heart of Earth

Heart of Heaven wanted humankind
to inhabit the four corners of the earth.
For several moons she wondered how to do it.
She tried all sorts of ways, but failed.
Then one day, Heart of Heaven stole
a small grain of maize from the Corn God
and covered it with her essence.
That little seed grew into a grain of human flesh.
The God of creation ordered the grindstone
to mash the grains of maize into a dough,
which tasted of heaven, promise and fertile nature.
Heart of Earth knew she needed to invent a way
of cooking the maize dough.
One day, she saw on the dress of
Heart of Heaven the perfectly round face of the moon.
She wondered how Heart of Heaven had shaped it
and decided that she must have flattened it
between her hands.
Heart of Earth copied the movement,
rounding and
flattening the balls of maize with her hands
until they resembled the face of the moon.
From that time forward we have fed on those
small moons which arise from the heat of the comal. *

* A comal is a cooking pot on which peasant families cook maize
tortillas which form part of their staple diet.

Agenda Cultural Comunica 1999
Honduras
translated and adapted by Judith Escribano/Christian Aid

The Little Shark

I was hurrying down the Via Dolorosa when I was halted by a request for help. Usually I can spot a sales pitch but I fell for this one. The jeweller's shop was closing. He could say 'clearance sale' but he could not spell it. Would I write it down so that he could put a notice in his window? I went in to write and I felt really sorry for him. Business was terrible now that there were no tourists. The shop was going to close. They were going to try and reopen it as a café for which the taxes were lower. His wife had just had a baby and they were hoping to sell off the stock as a start for the child. It did not take him long to persuade me to buy an amber bracelet for my mother. (I have to admit that it was a good and attractive bracelet and she was very pleased with it). I had not intended shopping that day but I felt pleased that I had helped a fellow being and bought an attractive gift.

The day before the Anglican representative had spelt 'clearance' so had the Baptist and the Welsh Independent and the Methodist.

Next day I returned to the shop with a camera. I told the young man that as well as being a minister I wrote for a religious magazine and said that I would tell the story of my purchase and publish a picture of his shop. He did not like the idea at all. He gave me some tea and suggested that he was only a little shark and that I should pursue the bigger sharks that infested the city.

Also, he told me a story which I am sure was true. The shop really was closing. He was an Armenian and planned to open a new shop in West Jerusalem where his customers would be Jewish inhabitants of the city rather than tourists. (He could do this but an Arab probably could not).

Business had been terrible. In the past he had not had to resort to tricks to entice people into the shop. There had been so many tourists. But now he had to use every possible stratagem to bring in the few customers who were around.

He was more inventive than some. But he was typical. The traders of Old Jerusalem are suffering real hardship. Many shops have closed and many more are in danger of doing so.

I said that I would not publish the picture of the shop but that I would tell the story as an illustration of the plight of the rather endearing sharks of Jerusalem.

Christopher Gillham
Wales

A Prayer Reflection

Lord,
        what a lot of sweat it takes to remake your world!

There's the sweat on the brow of the farmer ploughing an enormous field for a vast crop of the latest high tech super grain.
There's the sweat on the brow of the picker carefully harvesting coffee beans on a postage stamp of land high up in the Andes.
There's the sweat on the brow of the driver rushing to deliver milk to a super market hungry to fill its shelves.
There's the sweat on the brow of the fisherman watching the storm rolling towards a tiny boat in a big sea too far from land.
There's the sweat on the brow of the customs officer pocketing the latest bribe as sacks of food aid quietly vanish through the back door of a dockside warehouse.
There's the sweat on the brow of the logger waiting for the tree to topple but keeping an eye on the angry villagers protesting at the gates.
There's the sweat on the brow of the chief executive as the share price hits an all-time low and the deals done in secret topple into the light of popping flashguns.
There's the sweat on the brow of the children in a noisy shack in a forgotten corner where time is measured by how many shirts you make (and you never make enough).
There's the sweat on the brow of the village elders having to choose between cash crops for foreign markets and food for their people.

All these people, Lord,
        grafting and struggling, wheeling and dealing, dreaming and hoping.
And some of them are good whilst some are bad,
        some are seeking the best whilst some give in to the worst,
        some have a bold vision whilst some see only themselves.
But they're all your children, Lord.

And for all of them you sweated.

For there's sweat on the brow of a man from Nazareth hanging on a tree.
There's sweat in his eyes and sweat on his palms.
And he looks up to heaven as he carries the world in his heart,
        and quietly speaks for us all:

'Father, forgive them, they don't know what they're doing.'

Amen

Neil Thorogood
England

Fair Trade in Mauritius

Crafts, greetings cards, packaged flowers and organic cotton clothing are some of the products made at Craft Aid, which started in 1982 in the grounds of the Rose Hill Anglican Church in Mauritius.

Its vision was to provide creative and remunerative training and employment for young people, especially those with disabilities. The first two buildings housed a craft workshop and hostel. There were about twenty-five young people employed in the workshop — now about one hundred men and women have work at Craft Aid.

Christian-based Traidcraft was one of Craft Aid's first customers and is now their biggest customer for the alternative trade organisation (ATO) market.

Managing Director, Gaby Kamudu, describes the relationship. 'It has been a very enriching experience witnessing and experiencing ups and downs while improving our relationship as the years have gone by. We are so thankful for all the supports and helps, advice, recommendations and also punishments received throughout the years, which have really helped us to grow and supply a good service to our customers. Obviously, we still learn as we grow.'

During 1984 Craft Aid began negotiations with the Mauritius authorities and became the only small private organisation on the island to pack tea and sugar for export. A grant from Traidcraft helped to refurbish one end of the workshop and equip it to form the food-packing department. The work was deliberately labour intensive, to provide as much work as possible. By 1986 there were jobs for thirty-five young people.

Selling crafts is a risky business, and in 1987 Craft Aid had serious worries about having to lay people off during the quiet period. Fortunately the following year things were very different, as a large market had opened up for scale models of sailing ships. Craft Aid workers had developed the skills over previous years to take advantage of this opportunity.

'Now we can fly' – that was how Gaby described Craft Aid's success with sugar packing in the mid '90s. 'The work for Traidcraft had opened the door to a purely commercial client in Italy, as we are seen to be reliable. We are also going into the local market, with sugar packaging for a supermarket. We hope to have all year round employment for the twenty-five women and men in that department.'

Another development was organic cotton clothing, which came about when Carol Graham, a Traidcraft design consultant, visited in 1998. She explained: 'Their problem was they lacked information about what sort of styles, fabrics and colours would appeal to markets in the North. They had energy, enthusiasm and a great deal of skills they could draw on, but the lack of market awareness was a huge handicap.'

'It's very important when you're working with producers not to exclude them from the product development process. You have to give them the information that will make their product marketable. At times you have to be quite tough, but at the same time you have to be aware of the limitations they are working under and you have to allow space for their skills and cultural influences to come through. It's a matter of fine judgement and careful balance but in the end you have a product which reflects their skill and which is also attractive for the consumer.'

As Gaby said after Carol's visit: 'We are thankful for our first order. Together with Traidcraft we have been researching to bring it about. This is history! It is going to increase our work, making us more sustainable.'

Gaby says of the relationship with Traidcraft that we strongly feel we have a partnership relationship on which we can depend. A very good partner in Europe who supports us so that we in turn can help those under our care. I quote James 2 v 17: 'Even so faith if it has no works, is dead being alone'.

Traidcraft
England

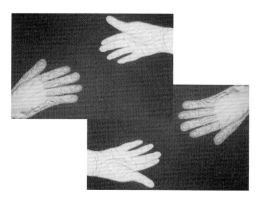

We Have a Job Because of You

La-ong is in her early thirties and lives in the village of Kwow-Si-Narin near Surin, in north-eastern Thailand. She is married with three children. Her husband has gone to Bangkok to seek work, so she has to support her family.

Her silver bead making is vital not just for daily living, but also to send her two sons, Ting and Tee, to school. Bead making is a skill that's passed on within families. The boys help out with the job of removing the resin from the finished beads, as do other members of the family.

La-ong's mother Kimhew Domhom lives nearby with her husband and their youngest daughter Dao who is thirteen and at school. Kimhew has helped to make beads for nearly 30 years. She concentrates mainly on working the family's land, which produces enough rice for the whole extended family.

La-ong has managed to buy a fridge to keep food fresh for them all. She says, 'Thank you for buying traditional craft from us. We have a job because of you.'

Many other people in the village make silver bead jewellery. The origins of these designs go back in the past to Nepal, but over the generations Kwow-Si-Narin bead makers have developed finer detail. Some families earn part of their living from subsistence farming and supplement this with jewellery making. Increasingly though it has become a major source of income.

The beads are made from high-grade silver leaf, shaped and then filled with a natural black resin. This allows for the delicate engraving, which follows, before the resin is removed by heating over boiling water and pushing it out with a needle. Dozens of beads may be needed to make one necklace.

As well as the bead makers, there are still one or two silversmiths with the skill to make exquisite, intricate silver flowers. The origin of the craft goes back over a thousand years, through the Khmer Empire to China and before that Nepal.

Puan Jiewthong takes two weeks or more to make a solid silver belt, decorated with flowers. At fifty-seven he would be happy to pass on his skill to youngsters in the area.' I am not at all possessive of my craft,' he says, 'but nobody wants to learn. So maybe I'll be the last one.' ThaiCraft is a fair trade marketing organisation that gives him an outlet through its monthly sales in Bangkok.

Marketing is vital and this is where ThaiCraft comes in, with both local sales and exports to fair trade organisations, like Traidcraft. Stephen Salmon the manager explains, 'The problem is that most non-governmental organisations (NGOs) are experienced in community development, not marketing. Too many NGOs encourage the production of local handicrafts only to face an awkward situation when it comes to selling them. If the village people know they can sell what they make, they'll feel motivated to put more effort into the production. That's the whole point of what we are trying to do. These people are artists, fine artists, and their work deserves a fair and appropriate reward.'

Traidcraft
England

For A Few Pence More

Guillermo Vargas Leiton is a 41-year-old Costa Rican who has a quiet, almost self-effacing air. 150 people in a room in Westminster, London, UK including a junior minister of state, were gripped by an eloquence that sprang from a passionate desire to communicate one world to another.

He described Coocafe, the coffee co-operative of which he is a part, and the role that Fairtrade plays in the life of its 4,000 members and their families. He said, 'When you buy our coffee you are not just buying our coffee but supporting our democracy.' These were not the words of a politician but of a man deeply involved with his community.

He explained, 'We are in a rural area, where our roads are not good; we need better water facilities; money to pay for our children to go to school. You might say the government should see to this. I say, yes, but they say they do not have the money. So you are helping us to make our choices every day.'

In 2001, Coocafe sold 1.4 tonnes of arabica beans, about 30 per cent of its crop, to the Fairtrade market. Most of its members have only one hectare of land and the majority live in the north of Costa Rica, one of the most marginalised areas. Vargas is clear that 13 years of fair trading has produced benefits which could not have been dreamt of without the Fairtrade premium.

'For my grandfather and my father, both coffee farmers, nothing changed.
Between 1950 and 1988, nothing got better. We knew we had good coffee, but working on our own, trading as individuals, we could do nothing. Then, in 1988, we decided to form a co-operative. It gave us strength to negotiate a better price and we were able to sell to Fairtrade. When we found that one thing had gone well by acting together, we tried other things.'

Coocafe, an umbrella organisation of nine smaller co-operatives, of which Vargas is general manager of one, has already proved itself creative in developing its capacities. Coocafe, was among the very first co-operatives to enter the Fairtrade system. It has gone a long way towards fulfilling the aims with which it started: to strengthen its producers in marketing, crop management, accounting and communication. Coffee that is not sold to Fairtrade, because there is as yet insufficient international demand for fairly traded coffee, is sold on the conventional export market, but at higher than normal prices because of the co-operative's increased knowledge of the trading system; a small proportion is also roasted for national consumption.

The group has made substantial investments in 'clean' technology, so that its processing plant has reduced water use by 80 per cent; a solar energy drying system for the green beans has put an end to the yearly logging of three hectares of forest; organic fertiliser is produced from the coffee pulp; and waste material from processing is disposed of safely, instead of being washed into local rivers. In the mid-Nineties Coocafe established the Cafe Forestal Foundation, which, using part of the Fairtrade premium, works on soil restoration, tree planting and environmental education in the wider region.

The co-op has provided almost 1,000 scholarships for farmers' children to go to secondary school and university; helped maintain local primary schools; developed income-generating schemes for women. Recently it purchased enough land to give 25 landless families plots. In effect, as well as farming advice, they have been given a long mortgage, which they will pay back as harvests allow. Like other co-op members, they will grow both food for themselves and crops other than coffee, such as macadamia nuts, cassava, yucca and bananas, which Coocafe also sells to ensure its members are not too dependent on coffee.

Gradually the co-operative is taking up organic methods, but it is a costly venture. Although in the long term, organic beans promise higher prices, it takes a minimum of three years without chemicals to gain certification. During that period the farmer has to control pests and weeds by labour-intensive means, at the same time as his harvest is reduced by up to half. 'We are talking about some people with income very, very low,' says Vargas. 'It is years of working, learning, experiencing some failures.'

Guillermo Vargas painted a vivid picture of a society slowly and patiently growing itself; inspired both by its own successes and, at least in part, by its contact with people in far-off places who buy the coffee it produces. 'We have to be proud about investing all that we have. We talk to consumers, asking for their support, needing their support, we come with self-respect.'

What a huge amount can be purchased for the sake of a few pence more.

The Fairtrade Foundation
England

Coffee is only one of eight products marketed by The Fairtrade Foundation. Other Fairtrade products include tea, chocolate/cocoa, bananas, honey, sugar, mangoes and orange juice.

Greening the Congregation

Eco-Congregation

What does an Eco-Congregation look like?

Eco-Congregation is an environmental programme that aims to encourage churches to consider environmental issues in their life and mission and enable them to make spiritual and practical responses.

The following stories are from churches seeking to live as Eco-Congregations ...

Through Word and Deed

The Eco-Congregation built their church upon a rock and:

Worshipped the God of Creation through word and deed.

Zion United Reformed Church is situated in the centre of Northallerton, a small town in North Yorkshire. Their Green Apostle, Liz Styan, described some of their work :

'As a church we were keen to expand our work on environmental issues as part of our mission. We had heard a little about Eco-Congregation and were really interested to find out how this could help us. We were sent a booklet outlining the programme. This included an 'environmental check-up' which helped us identify what we were already doing and prioritise what to do next. With guidance from some Eco-Congregation resources we have installed low-energy light bulbs and switched to using eco-friendly cleaning products. Creation is now mentioned with greater frequency in worship, and the green group led the initial service. We have been amazed and humbled at the response to our attempts at community involvement. Simply planting some trees and providing plants and bulbs for the gardens of a residential home has opened so many doors!'

Challenge for a Green Life Style

The Eco-Congregation built their church upon a rock and:

Challenged their members to green their personal lifestyle.

Rookhope is a small village in a remote part of Co. Durham with a United Anglican and Methodist Church. The church, which has around ten members, participated in the Eco-Congregation Pilot Study to discover what a small church in a rural area could achieve. The outcome was considerable! Initially the church explored creation issues through a Bible study series, their minister also took some environmentally themed assemblies in their local primary school and finally they spread good practice around their village. In one edition of their community newsletter they shared their environmental concerns and motivation and distributed it to every household with a free water hippo. A water hippo is a gel filled sachet designed for toilet cisterns that saves 1 litre of water per flush.

The Revd Penny Jones, Team Minister, St. John's Anglican & Methodist Church, Rookhope commented:

'*Our church valued the Eco-Congregation programme because: It brought us together, we had the chance to offer our own insights, it was fun! It gave us a new way to look at the Bible and it revitalised our relationship with God.*'

Premises Reflect Mission Priorities

The Eco-Congregation built their church upon a rock and:

Checked that their premises and life reflected their missionary priorities.

The Church of the Ascension, Ealing, was concerned about environmental issues, aware of their expensive heating system and keen to be good stewards of their property. Through Eco-Congregation, the Church commissioned an environmental consultation of their premises (free of charge from the Building Research Establishment).

The subsequent report included a series of phased recommendations:

- Immediate management and audit measures;
- Low-cost or short-payback period (less than 2 years);
- Medium cost or medium payback period (approx. 2-5 years);
- Work at refurbishment stage or with longer payback (approx. 5-10 years).

Gillian Harrison, the church's Green Apostle commented:

'The report was illuminating – it made us think about our energy use, how much we waste and how much we could save. We wish that we had known about having a professional audit six months earlier when a breakdown in our hall heating led us to replace the old electric system with a new electric one which we now realise is inefficient and expensive to run. However, now we have got the consultation report we are working our way through the recommendations and view it as our 'maintenance Bible' for our future programme of maintenance and repairs'.

Green Sermons and Green Decisions

The Eco-Congregation built their church upon a rock and:

Considered green theological perspectives in sermons and decisions.

Christchurch, Ross-on-Wye is a Methodist/United Reformed Church. They began their environmental project with special services at Harvest and One World Week and then sought to practice what had been preached. Initially a small co-ordinating green group was formed. Within a few months they had established a green Eco-Congregation notice board, started a recycling project and had collected three boxes of spectacles which were taken to a High Street optician to have a prescription reassignment prior to being shipped to Africa. The Church now has a monthly Traidcraft stall and is exploring working with young people on environmental issues.

The church's Green Apostle, Jean Pickering, commented: 'the latest venture that we have adopted is the 'Send A Cow' scheme designed to support agricultural development in Uganda. Through the scheme communities are provided with animals, training in husbandry, low-cost veterinary assistance and advice services when needed. We are hoping now to enthuse our sister churches in Ross and thereby the people of Ross to join us and together 'send a farm'.'

'Considering environmental issues in worship has prompted us to get involved in some practical projects that have really caught people's imagination. We have gained support from our members and interest from both our sister churches and the wider community in Ross. We feel that we are being led to care for God's creation and in small ways, to support the development needs of some of the poorest communities across the world.'

Wonder of God's Creation

The Eco-Congregation built their church upon a rock and:

Enthused their children with wonder for God's creation.

Kippen Church is situated on the main street of Kippen, a village in Scotland. Elaine McRae, who has responsibility for the childrens' work, devised a programme entitled 'Life in Biblical Times'. Through this the children explored the way in which people used and cared for the environment in Biblical times and compared these understandings with today's attitudes.

Elaine writes:

'*One of the first things that I wanted to discover was the way in which people related to natural materials in Biblical times. We invited a willow weaver to help tell the story of the infant Moses in the bulrushes, after which each of the children had a go at making a Moses basket. I'm sure that the children will remember the story and the fun of using natural materials, and hopefully they will have a greater sense of the value of natural materials.*'

Our next project is to plan with the children how we might turn an unused field at the back of the Kirk into a garden for the whole community, with a design telling biblical stories and using as many native species of plants as possible.'

Let's Get Real

The Eco-Congregation built their church upon a rock and:

Encouraged their young people to take environmental issues seriously.

First Ballymoney Presbyterian Church joined forces with Ballymoney District Council to get their Eco-Congregation Programme off the ground. They appointed their youth worker, Alex Patterson, as their Green Apostle to lead the church's environmental initiatives and be a link person with the Council.

Alex commented:

'Our young people quickly got stuck into the environmental work. They looked at creation issues through their Bible exploration sessions, adopted a piece of local authority land to do a mini Ground Force and undertook litter picking at our annual District day whilst wearing a tee shirt supplied by our Local Authority bearing the slogan: keep it green, keep it clean!'

Alex reflected:

'Following the Eco-Congregation Programme gave our youth programme a renewed sense of purpose. We felt that the church was taking an issue, that was important to us, seriously and being involved in Eco-Congregation boosted our faith and fellowship.'

Wildflowers for God

The Eco-Congregation built their church upon a rock and:

Planted their patch with wildflowers in praise of God.

Ruth Holdsworth tells the story of the EaRTH Group (Environmental and Resources Thinking) for the greening of Herringthorpe United Reformed Church, Rotherham, South Yorkshire, which began over ten years ago. The Church Meeting passed a statement of 'values' including the commitment to, 'have a practical concern for the community and the environment locally and worldwide.'

Our greening the church activities started when we were planning some building at our church. We were concerned to incorporate excellent environmental practice in our church extension. Since then the EaRTH Group has continued to prompt and guide the church to care for the environment in our church life and mission.

We invited the Brownies to help create a very small wildflower meadow in an L-shaped area of mown grass. In the autumn they planted wild flower plants grown from seed, and scattered a meadow seed mixture. By spring the strongest plants had established, so the grass was cut around them (with shears – it is a small area!). Several circles of grass were removed, and plantlets, which had been over-wintered in pots, were added. We talked about what we were doing and why, before the Brownies enthusiastically got to work. They are beginning to see this as their special area that they are helping to create. The following is the story in their words:

We planted flower because to bring Insect's back. I like planting flower (Danielle 8).

We planted some flower in a little area to help the Insect's eat and growe. We did a wetter area in a canen (corner) of our area (Kirsty Jane, 8).

We planted some wildflowers and plants to try and encorag butterflies, bugs and other wildlife. I think we have helped a lot of people because our children and our grandchildren will know all the different plants (Hannah 10).

Ruth continues…

'our EaRTH Group have stacked pruned branches so that they provide a wildlife habitat and rot down slowly to enrich the soil, planted a 'woodland edge' with a hedgerow, wild flowers and native bulbs, pruned neglected hedges in early spring after the berries have been eaten and before birds start nesting, to encourage them to thicken and become a more valuable wildlife habitat. In addition the hedges were under planted with a variety of native species including hawthorn, hazel, guelder rose, and blackthorn, and sited some bird boxes in strategic locations.

We hope that our church has set a good example of small, simple and effective steps that many of our church members and those within our local community who use the premises may replicate in their own gardens. To encourage this we have produced an attractive and colourful wall display highlighting what we have done to benefit wildlife and that it was done as a sign of our need to care for God's creation.'

Why are churches concerned with environmental issues?

Because of their belief in God 'maker of heaven and earth' and who calls us to act as good stewards to this gift.

Is Eco-Congregation an environmental and a mission programme?

Eco-Congregation developed through a pilot study. Churches reported that it helped them green their life, but working on environmental issues was enjoyable, boosted their church life and helped them engage effectively with their local neighbourhood.

Can churches really make a difference to the major environmental concerns facing the world?

If churches decide to green their life and mission, they may make a modest difference as a local church, but can make a significant difference by encouraging their members and the communities that they work with to adopt more environmentally sensitive lifestyles.

What does the Eco-Congregation Programme offer?

Eco-Congregation has three key components:

A set of resource modules designed to enhance church work.
Network support for churches.
An Award scheme to recognise and affirm excellence.

The resource modules cover the following topics:

Grounding in Faith

Module 1 Church check-up

> An aid to identifying a church's current environmental practice and developing priorities for action

Module 2 Celebrating creation!

> Ideas and resources for worship

Module 3 Creation and Christianity

> Some green theological perspectives

Growing in Faith

Module 4 Acorn to oaks

> Ideas and activities for children's work

Module 5 Tread gently – go green

> Ideas and activities for youth groups

Module 6 Exploring God's green word

> An address and two sets of studies for House Groups

Managing in Faith

Module 7 Greening the cornerstone

> Guidelines on caring for church premises

Module 8 Greening the purse strings

> Management of financial, catering and purchasing matters

Module 9 Planting and conserving Eden

> Practical ideas and advice to care for church grounds and land

What a World

Living in Faith

Module 10 Green Choices

Information and suggestions to green personal lifestyles

Module 11 Community Matters

Ideas to help churches work with, through and for their local community

Module 12 Global Neighbours

Sources and resources to help Churches' think globally and act locally.

How can I start to green the life of my church?

The Eco-Congregation Introduction Pack includes a 'churches check-up' which is designed to help churches identify and affirm what they are already doing and to prioritise what they would like to tackle. They can then select resource modules, which are free of charge, to help them achieve their own objectives. Churches can order these by completing the Registration Form, which requires the agreement of a church decision-making meeting.

Who is behind Eco-Congregation?

Eco-Congregation is a partnership between the Environmental Issues Network of Churches Together in Britain and Ireland and the environmental charity ENCAMS (formerly Going for Green and the Tidy Britain Group).

Have you anything to offer Black-Majority Churches?

Yes! ENCAMS has received support from DTLR to run and develop an environmental programme especially for Black-Majority Churches.

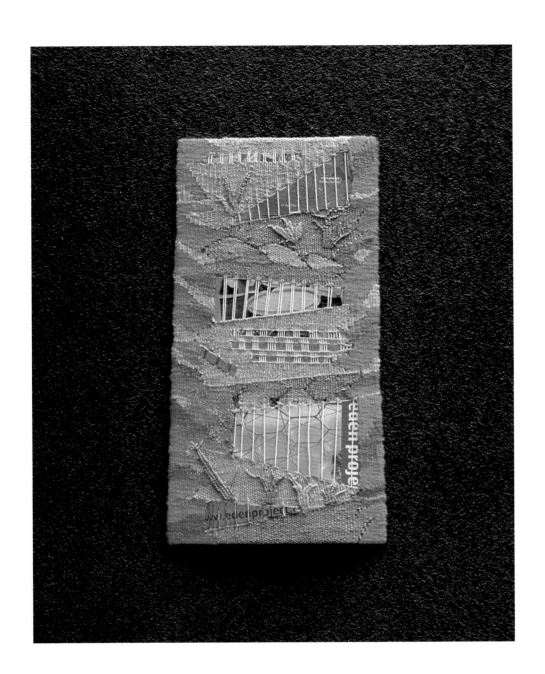

Make Justice Grow

Share the Harvest

God of compassion,
I see him now,
Torn shirt, no shoes,
My brother.

Our lives meet in the global market
Woven together in the web of trade.

But he's hungry,
He touches my heart
And I ache to understand,
To share his life,
His laugh, his dance.

God of compassion and justice,
May your harvest be more fairly shared,
And may such hunger change my heart.

Linda Jones
England

Lament of a Consumerist

When I see a green tree crying
and hear a mute fish dying,
Move me from selfishness to sharing
to watching and caring.

When I feel a neighbour sighing
and know that I am life denying,
Move me from selfishness to sharing
to loving and caring.

When I smell sick sky, sick sea, sick earth, sick all
and taste living water dying,
Move me from selfishness to sharing
to healing and caring.

Erna Colebrook
England

Share My Lunch

Ramesh is always smiling! He is fourteen years old and spends his life in a wheelchair. I first met him at the Association for People with Disability (APD) where he attends school. APD provides transport to the school each day for some of the children who live in one of the nine slum ghettos in Bangalore, south India.

I had learned on a previous visit that the children are given a good square meal each lunch time. To my amazement the cost was only £8.00 per day to provide meals for 120 children.

A few months later I returned to Bangalore with £750 in travellers cheques for the children's meals. It cost about 50p to change the cheques and I took 50,000 rupees to N S Hema, the honorary general secretary and founder member over forty years ago, of APD. Hema responded, 'Oh Geoff meals for 100 days for the children.' Afterwards I was visiting parts of the campus and met Ramesh at lunchtime. His plate contained rice, greens, a chapatti and his sweet for pudding. We were talking about his school life and hopes for the future when he just looked up and said 'Will you have some of my lunch?'

Geoffrey Duncan
England

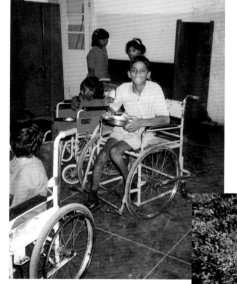

Ramesh with his lunch

Profound Moments

Recently, I had the pleasure of visiting a Congregational church in Argentina. This church, in the small town of Jardin America, was challenged some years ago by the desperate poverty in the sizeable shanty town in the surrounding area. They worked with the inhabitants of the shanty town and over the years, have established a school and clinic, a worshipping church and a garden where people can grow their own produce. On Sundays, the people offer and receive gifts of bread and rice. The gifts are held up in the service to be blessed, and are then distributed to the poorest people in the town, often providing the last bastion against starvation.

On the Sunday that I was there, to my astonished gratitude, one of the local men called me forward and publicly offered a bag of rice, 'for the homeless children in your own church'. Union Chapel, my church, runs a drop in centre for homeless people, including women and children as well as men. For my own part, I was deeply moved, and carried the rice back to London, where I presented it to the drop-in centre on the following Sunday.

This was a profound moment. The volunteers and workers in the drop-in, many of them homeless or ex-homeless people, stood in shared silence as they received the news of the gift. Later, I heard that they wanted to reach out to the poor of Argentina. They wanted to take a collection to send, to support the work being done.

Me, I was just a mediator. This was the destitute of the world reaching out to each other. Poor people recognising each other's need, and sharing each other's dignity, in the act of giving and receiving gifts. Fantastic.

Janet Wootton
England

Tip the Balance

Tip the balance in favour of the poor
Lighten the load of those weighed down
Level out inequality
Distribute warehouse mountains
Share out wealth
Which was never ours to hoard
Turn the tables
On those who play the markets

Stock pile generosity
Measure in hope
Sell shares in selfishness
Settle for dividends of solidarity

For added value
Build up a portfolio in justice
Invest in the growth of the kingdom of God

Build up trust
Act in faith
Risk security and comfort to find a richer life

Attend to our needs
And shop wisely
See trade as an encounter, an opportunity to engage
Above all else, let our interest be in people.

Sophie Stanes
England

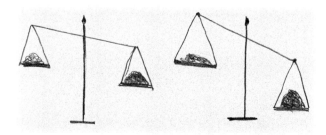

Daily Offerings

Walking back to the farm,
I saw a ute * and trailer,
being mobbed by Mums,
black and white
distraught and mooing.
The daily offering
of new born calves
were being taken away
in the trailer
to be sorted.
Heifer, bull, bobby,**
long life, short life, no life.
A daily offering
laid on the altar
of profit,
big business,
the sainted Dairy Board.

If the people of New Zealand
were starving
we might be justified
in induced abortions
the killing of tiny calves
that don't fit farm timetables.
But this is not a place
where people starve en masse.
On the contrary
there is so much meat and dairy
we are dying of excess!

Consumer demand!
The export trade!
And as dairy farmers say,
'If you want, milk, cheese, butter, then …'
Consumers are waking up
realising the power
of their wallets, beginning to say,
'Not at any price, not anymore.'

Each one of us counts
in the choices we make.

What of the future?
What diabolical inheritance
might we leave,

in land worn out,
polluted waterways,
resistant bugs?
What is the human cost
for people who work in this way?
We look back with disdain
at ancient people
who made daily offerings
of animals and birds
killed and burned
to appease angry gods.
Are we any different?
We still make daily offerings
to placate a different god.

*   *a ute is a farm truck*
**   *a bobby is a calf, slaughtered at 2 - 4 days for hide and meat*

Wendy D Ward
Aotearoa New Zealand

Seeds of the Kingdom

I turn towards the light
Like the plant on a sill
Reaching for a glimpse of the truth of hope

I raise my head to the sun
Like the crops in the earth
Scanning for the warmth of your compassion

I sway and seek the freshening rain
Unsure of my direction
Seeking to remember the waters of my baptism

Like the mustard tree
My branches stretch to shelter
Reaching for the ways to do your work

Compassionate God you know me
Hold me and direct me
Show me how to water the seeds of your kingdom.

Linda Jones
England

Twenty Years On

It is forecast that by 2025, due to the increase in the population of the world,
two-thirds of the people will live in cities.
There will be immense suffering because of
poverty,
crime,
lack of health care,
                    including physically and mentally impaired people,
serious housing shortages
                    increases in slum dweller ghettos,
climate change,
                    drought and flood
the increased plight of itinerant migrant workers,
lack of education.

Women, girls and children will make up 70% of the estimated
1.3 billion people living in these conditions.

Geoffrey Duncan
England

Before you finish your breakfast you will have depended upon half the world.

Martin Luther King
USA

Loving God, Creator of Earth and Heaven

Loving God, Creator of Earth and Heaven,
You are holy.
We are called to build your Kingdom of Peace
through Justice for the whole Creation.
Nourish us daily through the fruits of the earth
and forgive us our destructiveness of Nature,
as we accept its effects upon us.
Help us not to be short-sighted
but to live sustainable
lives without greed.
The world in its glory belongs to you,
who loves and lets live,
for all time.
Amen

Martyn Goss
England

What a World

The Last House

The last house in the road now stands
challenging meadows with brooding greed
produced by the town's desperate need
on the tips of those outstretched grasping hands:

but wander beyond – for here is the place
where horses canter and kites are flown
and cares can be lost and overgrown
as the lark bubbles upward in liquid space.

This is the way that the lovers amble,
where willow-herbs in their beards of grey
doze by the sorrel rusting away
protected by barbed-wire of fruited bramble;

but where is defence from a lorry's load?
So the fields ask, and their lives depend
on the answer here at the town's end –
How long will that be the last house in the road?

Cecily Taylor
England

Great Trees

I don't know anything more splendid, Lord,
than the great tree on the hillside,
its roots grasping rock,
snaking across the path;
its trunk a smooth column, rock solid,
and its crown up there scraping the clouds
making me look upward.
It is as though you sowed a giant garden
full of majesty and shade and quiet strength.

> With a metallic scream
> in an hour
> all that lies dead
> sent on its way to the mill
> and the hillside is bare, bereft.

Give us the mind of the Maker
to treasure the work of your hands.
Humanity as Giver not Taker
may share your creativity plans.

Bernard Thorogood
Australia

God of Creation

God of creation,
and mystery,
and holiness,
may your will and your ways
of justice and peace
permeate our lives
here and now
as well as ever after.
Feed us today
and forgive our debts and wrongs
while we forgive those indebted
and wrongful to us.

Help us not to be tempted
by what denies your love.
But free us from that
which separates us
from you and from each other.

The glory and the power and
the way belong to you.
Now and forever.
Amen

Martyn Goss
England

Prayers for Fair Values

We think of the people involved in the production of the coffee that we can smell.
We pray for the coffee growers in Africa and Latin America who are suffering huge
losses in income due to the crash in world market prices and cannot afford even to
buy food for their children. We pray for justice for farming communities
everywhere and give thanks for the initiatives that support them such as the
Fairtrade Mark.

We pray for all those who work in factories throughout the world, manufacturing
the good that we take for granted,
from Indian sweatshops to hi-tech plants in this country.
Where people face lives of pitiful wages and long working hours,
we ask for their liberation and pray for their health and safety.

We pray for all those who import and sell the products we buy, that they will have
a sense of their responsibilities. We ask that you grant them courage to take a
stand against exploitation and the wisdom to pay producers the true value of their
work.

The Fairtrade Foundation
England

The Cry for Our Poor

Paper on the streets
paint on the walls
cans and empty bottles
left where they fall,
don't care shows
car's not taxed
abandoned in rows
glass on the seat
ripped up, poor,
feel so bad
way beyond the law.
Nothing can reach
heart of shame
who can teach
who will show
which way to turn.
Broken branches
left to die
pulled from the tree,
confronted they lie
I didn't do it
I don't care
you can't make me
learn to share
responsibility
for this world,
my despair's
much too deep
you can't see
I can't feel
don't you know
nothing's real.
You taught me
info techno,
mobile phone, no
cultured ways,
text addiction,
disposable life,

believing fiction's
real life.
Drugs alcohol
not the only fix
shopping, shopping
never enough,
channel hopping
never finding
food
you're craving
deep inside.
All those adverts,
yes they lied.
nothing can give you
nothing satisfy
till you stop,
let your soul cry,
help me find
peace of mind.

Pat Randall
England

Gleanings

Our Recycling Bins

It is only possible to recycle paper up to eight times and after that the fibres are destroyed.
Glass can be recycled ad infinitum.
Our drink cans can be recycled indefinitely.

The Cost of Travel

Everyone enjoys going on holiday particularly to places far away. However, air travel has a hidden cost because it is a major source of atmospheric pollution. Air traffic has doubled in the last fifteen years and pollution fromplanes is an increasing problem. Although planes are becoming cleaner and more efficient all the time,plane pollution cannot be stopped completely,

Water Needed for Life!

According to the United Nations more than one billion people have no access to improved water supplies; they draw their water from potentially contaminated sources.
'Water comes before food', says a woman from Ghana 'water is expensive taking almost all my daily income.'
By 2025, the number of people facing water shortage will increase to 63% of the world's population.

Scuttling Around the Namibian Desert

Scuttling around the Namibian desert is thirsty work! Finding a drink is no easy matter when the rainfall is less than one hundred millimetres a year. The local beetle population has learned to survive in such extreme conditions by extracting water from desert fog! Scientists are looking at ways of developing this technique for struggling farmers in rain-starved parts of the world. The unique surface of the beetle's back attracts water molecules in the fog, allowing them to settle and form droplets that will roll down the insect's back and into  its mouth. Scientists found that the surface could be copied and reproduced in sheet form through techniques such as injection moulding and printing to produce structures that can collect water for drinking and farming.

Island Treasures

Madagascar has been likened to a giant ant. The country has many unique species of plants and animals, including twelve families of plants, which are only found on the island. Since humankind came to Madagascar some two thousand years ago almost 90% of its natural primary vegetation has disappeared. Urgent help is needed to prevent imminent extinction through habitat loss because of the activities of horticultural collectors.

The Dodo

The Dodo became extinct in 1680 – how many more since then?

The African Willow

Compounds extracted from an African willow tree could be included in medical research as an anti-cancer drug.

Lemon Snow

In cold places, winter air pollution produces acid snow that can taste as sour as a lemon.

Car Parking Charges *

It costs less than the car parking charge for a day at a London Underground station to provide for one month:

- assistance toward training two health workers in Bangladesh;

- 670 seedlings every year to be planted by Ethiopian farmers to help re-green their land;

- enough tools for villagers in Sudan to dig a well and give the whole community a permanent supply of clean, safe water.

* £2.50 per day

Geoffrey Duncan/Pamela Pavitt
England

A Story for Our Time

Once upon a time there was a large and powerful school bully. He tried to run things his way, especially in the playground – teasing and cajoling the other boys and girls he felt superior to. One of his tricks was to offer goodies to his fellows in return for favours – even money. Once he gave a large bag of sweets to a group of children as long as he could have their support if he got into trouble. In many ways the bully was nice and affable, but beneath the surface lay a sense of arrogant domineering.

Then one day he produced a box of fireworks and showed these off to everyone else. If things didn't go his way, he gently suggested, he had means of being particularly unpleasant. After a while it was discovered he had passed on a few small fireworks to some of the other schoolground bullies. He didn't mind if they used these to menace their friends, especially if they continued to give him status and regular gifts.

However, some of those who obtained fireworks really did not like the bully at all and vowed to get their own back. They watched him and learned from him. One day a particular gang of boys with a threatening reputation actually fired a small rocket directly at the bully and struck his leg. This caused him such great pain and outrage that he vowed to have them removed from school. He got as many of the other pupils on his side as he could and set off to seek them out with all his fireworks, for they were somewhere hidden in the huge school grounds, which he didn't really know.

Meanwhile, some realised that the bully would not remain strong and rich forever and waited, looking for their own time …

Martyn Goss
England

Help Counter Global Warming

The Council for World Mission's (CWM) churches called on its recent Council to be more involved in the campaign to halt global warming, which threatens to destroy their lands.

'We, the Pacific people, are the most vulnerable to global warming,' said Eti Kine, the president of Ekalesia Kelisiano Tuvalu. 'We've experienced major climate change in the past five years.'

Greenhouse gases lead to a rise in the earth's temperature, melting the ice caps and increasing the sea level. Large areas of many Pacific islands are now under water. Other parts have been damaged by the extreme weather – cyclones, hurricanes and droughts – sparked by global warming.

Jacques Matthey, the representative of the World Council of Churches (WCC) at CWM's Council and the co-ordinator of its Mission and Evangelism Team, said the WCC was campaigning on behalf of its churches, 'But there's been a major shift in the international political environment with the victory of George W Bush,' the US president, who is pulling his country out of the Kyoto agreement aimed at cutting the greenhouse gas emissions.

'Bush's decision is proof that developed countries don't care,' said Willie Star, the general secretary of the Nauru Congregational Church. The Pacific seems too insignificant and far away for them, he added.

The CWM family can make a difference, said Winnie Tsitsi, the secretary of the Women's Group of the Nauruan Church. 'We need the solidarity of this assembly to make global warming a real issue. We, the Pacific people, count.'

Council for World Mission

A Pacific Context

Pacific islands, which could vanish forever if global temperatures continue to rise, are already suffering as rising sea levels swallow surrounding islets and contaminate drinking water.

Rising sea levels have already endangered sacred sites and drowned some small islands off Kiribati and Tuvalu, including the islet of Tebua Tarawa, once a landmark for Tuvalu fishermen. Kiribati has already had to move roads inland on its main island as the Pacific Ocean has eaten into the shore. The Kiribati Protestant Church has a project building sea walls and raising awareness locally. Members of the Ekalesia Kelisiano Tuvalu are also working hard to highlight the issue locally and internationally.

Leaders argue that people living in rich countries would feel a greater sense of urgency about stopping global warming if they ran the same risk of being drowned or running out of fresh water as do Pacific islanders. They fear for the future of their traditional homes and unique cultures.

'These days we seem to get flooding every time it rains for more than hour or two. This is very unusual. It causes many problems for us – it is very bad in the villages, most of which are at sea level,' says Rev Paulo Koria, General Secretary, Congregational Christian Church in Samoa.

A healthy, thriving environment is vital to the survival of the many vibrant indigenous cultures of the Pacific.

Leigh Bredenkamp
Aotearoa New Zealand

Global Market

Across cyberspace
figures tumble
plucked
from the air
invisible jungle

Incomprehensible numbers
of lives
trapped
on the net
lifted
dropped.com
in a moment of exchange.

Linda Jones
England

A Maori Perspective

Air is viewed as a *taongo* (treasure) derived from *Ranginui* (the sky father). Maori legend tells that following the separation of *Ranguini* and *Papatuanuku* (the earth mother) their child *Tawhirimatea* fled with *Ranguini* to his new home in the sky. From there *Tawhirimatea* controls the wind and elements. Air pollution degrades and lessens the *mauri* or life-force of this *taonga*. It also affects the *mauri* of other *taonga*, for example, plants and animals, as all living things need air and all things share the same air. It's important to Maori to protect and maintain the *mauri* of *taonga*.

Maori are concerned about the health effects of the increasing emission of contaminants into the air, depletion of the ozone layer and high levels of solar radiation. They are also concerned about the effects air pollution has on:

- Customary resources – plants and animals require clear and pure airways. Native plants provide food and natural medicines.

- The moon, stars and rainbows are important in Maori mythology. The stars are particularly important as they represent the generations that have passed into the night. The movements of the moon and the lunar calendar help tell the time of year for sowing and harvesting.

- The spiritual values of *waahi tapu* (sacred places) and other *taonga*.

Leigh Bredenkamp
Aotearoa New Zealand

One Single World

One single world
With tens of races
And hundreds of nations
In thousands of places
With millions of families
And billions of faces,
Yet this but a fraction
Of God's mega-graces
In billions of stars
Over millions of seasons
Showing thousands of mysteries
Yet hundreds of reasons
For tens of love-laws
Uniting creation.

David J Harding
England

Work for the Peace of the City

Work for the Peace (the shalom) of the city ... pray to the Lord on its behalf, since on its peace yours depends ... (Jer 29:7 NJB)

In 586 BCE Jerusalem was laid waste by the Babylonian army under Nebuchadnezzar. The majority of the population, including all the professional classes were taken into exile in Babylon. A short while later Jeremiah wrote to the exiles urging them to settle down in Babylon, build up the life of the Jewish community there, and (astonishingly) to work for shalom, the peace and well-being, of Babylon.

Peace to the city,
shalom for Babylon.
Peace to the Temple desecrators
and the exile-makers,
shalom on the zigurrat of the sun-god and those who believe
that his is the true reality.

Surely you don't mean it Lord?
Surely your blessing is for us, your faithful few?

My child, love your enemies and pray for those who persecute you.
Hatred diminishes
envy poisons
and fear cripples,
your peace and theirs are one.

But Lord,
we are your chosen ones,
elected to walk in your path
and they have dragged us from it,
severed us from the umbilical cord of the Temple,
quenched the fires of sacrifice.
How can you ask us to pray for peace?

My child
I weep with you by Babylon's waters
for my heart is broken by your pain,
yet my tears flow too for those who
dominate and destroy,
blind to my light
deaf to my symphony,
caught in spirals of delusion and violence.

You,
my weak ones,
my little ones,
can craft their salvation from your steadfast vulnerability.
Your peace and theirs are one.

So be it Lord,
hear our prayer for mighty Babylon
for our peace and hers are one
in your rich economy of your blessing.
Lead us to the land of milk and honey
where lion lies with lamb and ox with bear,
and Babylonian and Jew party together
in the light of a rainbow
and a boy baby lies in the arms of a mother distracted by crosses.
Amen

David G Cornick
England

Arms Trade and the Environment

(This article develops ideas originally explored in CAAT NEWS, a bi-monthly publication of London-based Campaign Against Arms Trade)

The arms trade casts shadows across the world. Understandably, direct loss of human life from what are, after all, products designed to be instruments of violence, takes centre place for anti-militarist movements. More recently, however, concern has spread to the environmental impact of production and trading of armaments.

It is well documented how wars leave specific legacies of environmental degradation. In Vietnam, where Agent Orange was dispersed in huge amounts as a defoliant, the environment was the deliberate and intended target to facilitate American air attacks on people. The burning oil wells of Kuwait and the depleted uranium-tipped shells of Iraq, Kosovo and now Afghanistan are other, more recent examples of military-generated environmental damage.

But the problem reaches far beyond the actions of military forces and their technologies in direct combat situations. Arms dumping has created toxic hotspots around the world. Hazardous releases result from the production of armaments and other military goods, even those without chemical or nuclear components. For example, the processing of heavy metals at arms factories is associated with groundwater and soil contamination as well as hazards to the workers who come in contact with them.

Testing technologies within military research and development programmes impacts on the environment too. So does the dismantling of withdrawn or superceded products (when they are not sold on to developing countries). The fate of the United States' chemical warfare stockpile is a case in point. By 1999 America possessed some 30,000 tons of chemical weapons, including deadly nerve and blister agents. Congress has ordered the destruction of most of them as part of an international treaty. Critics of the incineration disposal arrangements point to the hazards they create. Dioxins and other toxins including arsenic, lead and mercury are released when the weapons and their containers are burned. These pose a range of known dangers including cancer, immune system disorders, neurological damage and birth defects.

Raytheon, a company already notorious among anti-arms trade activists, is in line to build and run incinerators in Oregon as part of this disposal programme. Defense contractor EG and G Defense Materials oversee operations at a similar facility in Tooele County. Often it is the corporate beneficiaries of arms production who also capitalise on disposal when their products are no longer required.

Military pollution, like war itself, disproportionately impacts on the already disadvantaged. Poor communities across the world bear the brunt of dumping and burning programmes. Developing countries are key buyers in an arms trade overwhelmingly centred on 'first world' corporations. They are also the prime victims of military pollution. Chronically contaminated expanses of land and unexploded munitions in Panama, the Philippines and Korea, among many other degraded places, are part of the cost of inflated, mainly 'first world' shares in this uniquely wasteful industry.

A similar pattern exists within the wealthier countries. The United States, for example, has a tradition of pushing disposal arrangements onto Amerindian lands, compounding a historical injustice with slow poisoning of indigenous people. Within as well as between countries, the poor are expected to live with the most damaging bi-products of wealth in general and of the military sector in particular. The social geography of the production, distribution and consumption of miltary products ensures that environmental mayhem and social injustice are mutually reinforcing.

The agendas of governments and corporations, however, do not always go uncontested. A citizens' coalition, the Military Toxics Project (MTP) was formed last summer to challenge the polluting activities of the US armed forces. MTP supports congressional steps to remove exemptions from safety and environmental legislation long enjoyed by the US Department of Defense. It opposes hazardous waste generation from testing and use of toxic munitions. Its component organizations campaign against nuclear propulsion as well as incineration of the chemical stockpile.

In developing countries also there are encouraging precedents. Grassroots and community groups have developed imaginative and sometimes effective approaches to resisting the arms trade environmental juggernaut. November 2000 saw the gathering in San Diego of community activists including delegates from the Caribbean as well as North America and Japan to pool experiences and develop strategies for calling the polluters to order. These pioneering efforts deserve support and extension internationally.

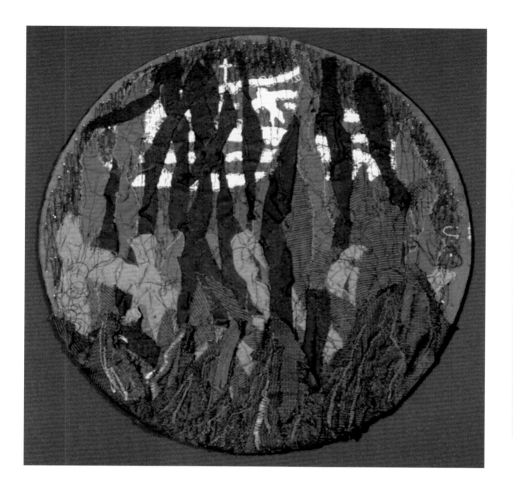

Demilitarization of economy and society includes promotion of relatively safe methods of disposal for existing armaments. The various national and regional branches of the increasingly globalized arms trade have created their own local hotspots and hazards. Many of these remain unchallenged and require substantial independent research. This is in addition to pollution created by arms trade products at the point of military use.

The problems, moreover, are set to worsen further. Decreasing global spending on armaments in the years after the collapse of the Soviet Union had already bottomed out by 1998. As the Stockholm International Peace Research Institute annual report 2001 revealed, by 1999 the graph was pointing upward once again. 11th September, 2001 gave a massive boost to planned growth, centred on the United States weapon development and marketing bonanza. The return to Cold War rates of arms proliferation threatens further escalation of assaults on both people and the environment.

Raytheon, the Carlyle Group, BAe Systems, Lockheed Martin and the rest see great commercial potential in President Bush's 'war on terrorism' and these are not the sort of people to let opportunities pass by.

The dealers in death routinely appeal to patriotism to justify their activities. Certainly it is true that states promote and facilitate the arms trade through subsidies and export guarantee arrangements. Moreover, since its inception in 1947 the General Agreement on Tariffs and Trade (GATT) has favoured war production by providing cover for state support. GATT's general mission is to create a world of free markets for goods and services. Its provisions are designed to encourage or force removal of what is seen as government interference in the market. The arms trade, however, is alone exempted from the GATT regime. Article XX1 of GATT allows that governments may define their own 'essential security interests' and protect them by such means as subsidies. As the body charged with administering GATT, the World Trade Organisation plays a key and fatal role ensuring that war will follow war.

Alert to issues raised by contemporary social and environmental movements, some friends of the arms trade are now developing a sophistry of 'environmentally friendly weapons'. It is worth remembering that the same business interest groups consistently market assurances about civilian-friendly 'smart bombs' that are contradicted by each new military adventure. Weaponry remains a mounting threat to both human life and the environment which sustains it. A mind-set which promotes the means of military aggression will also find ways to menace the broadest conditions of life. Equally, curbing the right to pollute now exercised by the armed forces of the world and their associated industries unfolds a challenge to militarism at all levels. Opposition to that right contains the potential to enlarge the struggle for peace in areas where people work and try to live.

David Binns
England

A Litany for Forgiveness

'The arms trade casts shadows across the world' (David Binns)

Across the shadow cast by the production of weapons
  let us shine the light of love,
    that those who imagine ways to kill
      may turn to Life for their creative vision.

Across the shadow cast by the testing of weapons
  let us shine the light of mercy,
    that the planet and all it sustains
      may be cruelly violated no longer.

Across the shadow cast by the trading of weapons
  let us shine the light of protest,
    that the wretched of the earth
      may be exploited no further.

Across the shadow cast by the dismantling of weapons
  let us shine the light of care-fulness,
    that soil, air, water and all life-resources
      may be polluted and spoiled no more.

Across the shadow cast by our un-owned darkness
  let us shine the light of truth,
    that we may befriend our fears
      and stop projecting them on to others.

God, forgive us
Our disconnection
From the wholeness and holiness
Of your creation.

God, forgive us
Our despoiling
Of so much that is still unfolding
From your vision for the earth.

God, forgive us
Our violation
Of the poorest and the least
Whom you love the most.

God, forgive us
Our grasping
For power and profit
At the expense of your 'little ones'.

God, forgive us
Our brutalizing
Of our own hearts, souls and spirits:
Break us, and re-make us to reflect your love.

We join our hands with those
  whose hands burst through the chains of
    exploitation.
We join our hearts with those
  whose hearts overflow with indignation
    against injustice.
We join our spirits with those
  who offer spirited resistance to death-
    dealing forces.

Kate Compston
England

Resources

A Rocha
The Revd Dave Bookless,
13 Avenue Road,
Southall,
Middlesex
UB1 3BL

Email: uk@arocha.org
Website: www.arocha.org

Action Aid
Hamlyn House
Macdonald Road
Archway
London
N19 5PG

Email: mail@actionaid.org.uk
Website: www.actionaid.org

Basic Needs
158A Parade,
Leamington Spa,
Warwickshire
CV32 4AE

Email: basicneeds@basicneeds.org.uk
Website: www.basicneeds.org.uk

Campaign Against the Arms Trade
and
Christian Campaign Against the Arms Trade
11 Goodwin Street
London
N4 3HQ

Christian Ecology Link
George Dent
20 Carlton Road
Harrogate
North Yorks
HG2 8DD

Email: cel2000@christian-ecology.org.uk
Website: www.christian-ecology.org.uk

Council for World Mission
Ipalo House
32/34 Great Peter Street
London
SW1P 2DB

Email: council@cwmission.org.uk
Website: www.cwmission.org.uk

Earth Summit
United Nations
Environment and Development
(UNED)
3 Whitehall Court
London
SW1A 2EL

Eco-congregations
The Rev David Pickering
Elizabeth House
The Pier
Wigan
WN3 4EX

Email: ecocongregation@encams.org
Website: www.encams.org/ecocongregation

Intermediate Technology Development Group
The Schumacher Centre for Technology and Development
Bourton-on-Dunsmore
Rugby
CV23 9BR

Website: www.itdg.org

Survival International
6 Charterhouse Buildings
London
EC1M 7ET

Email: info@survival-international.org
Website: www.survival-international.org

The Fairtrade Foundation
Suite 204
16 Baldwin's Gardens
London
EC1N 7RJ

Email: mail@fairtrade.org.uk;
Web site: www.fairtrade.org.uk

Traidcraft
Kingsway North,
Gateshead,
NE11 0NE

Website: www.traidcraft.co.uk

Author Index

Titles

A Cameo of Creation

Get Wise!

Let All Creation Dance and Sing

Global Perspectives

To Earn Our Rice and Bread

Greening the Congregation

Make Justice Flow

Acknowledgements

Creation Care, Environmental Issues network, CTBI
Communion and Creation © Elizabeth Welch

A Cameo of Creation

Beauty and Compassion © David Pickering
Bless the Lord © Jenny Spouge
Blessing for the Earth © Edward P Echlin
Cameo of Nature, A © Grace Westerduin
Children's Song © David Mowbray
Coconut Tree © Sun-Ai Lee Park
Collect, A © David Pickering
Creation and Destruction © Grace Westerduin
Creation Thoughts © Pamela Pavitt
Dawn-Light, The © David J Harding
Desert Bloomed, The © Brian Savage
For the Beauty of All Creation © Kevin Fray
God Has Given © Colin Ferguson
Hug for the Trees, A © Eleanore Milardo
Litany of Air, Sea and Earth, A © Heather Johnston
Litany of Celebration for Our Creation, A © Neil Thorogood
Meditation, A © Neil Thorogood
Mission and Witness © David Pickering
One Flower © David J Harding
Our Offering © David Pickering
Parable of the Bougainvillea, The © Jenny Spouge
Partners in Creation © Heather Johnston
Poppies © Marjorie Dobson
Prayer of Intercession, A © Neil Thorogood
Prayer of Praise, A © Neil Thorogood
Prayer of Thanksgiving, A © Pat Randall
River, The © Margot Arthurton
Rural and Real © David J Harding
Solomon's Glory © Bernard Thorogood
Song for All God's Creatures, A © William Whitson
Song of Love, A © William Whitson
Song for Our Town, A © William Whitson
Song of The Charente © Margot Arthurton
Song of the Seasons, A © William Whitson
Summer Pasture © Cecily Taylor
Thank You for Plants © Pamela Pavitt
Thought of Trees, A © Cecily Taylor
Visitor © Cecily Taylor
We Gaze in Wonder at the Morning's Dawning, Andrew Pratt © Stainer and Bell Ltd.,
Words A Waterfall © Eleanore Milardo
World Belongs to God, The – Source Unknown
You Placed Us On This Earth – Source Unknown

Get Wise!

Aboriginal Culture © Sister Rosita Shiosee, World Council of Churches,
Animals and Plants are Creatures, Too © Edward P Echlin
Benedicite © David Mowbray
Creation © Marjorie Dobson
Creator Lord of Planet Earth © David Mowbray
Earth is the Lord's, The © David Hallman
From Garbage Dump to Healthy Living © Geoffrey Duncan
Greed © Eleanore Milardo
Green Song © Liz Sharma
Litany of Praise, A © Neil Thorogood
Lord of the Wonder of Creation © Geoffrey Duncan
Lord Have Mercy © Peter Graystone
Oh God We Know © Elizabeth Gray-King
Pathway Through Recent Centuries © Pamela Pavitt
Peace Process © Cecily Taylor
Prayer of Confession, A © Neil Thorogood
Sidwell's Story © Martyn Goss
Simplistic? © Margot Arthurton
Stewards of Your World, an extract from the hymn This is Our Prayer © Cecily Taylor
That Relentless Rush © David Mowbray
This Is Our Home © Colin Ferguson
Toxic Lifestyles © Linda Jones/CAFOD
Water © Janet Lees
Water Gets Dirty © Association for People with Disability, Bangalore, south India
Wise One, The © Cecily Taylor

Let All Creation Dance and Sing

Aammiq: A Special Place © Chris Walley
As Dawn is Breaking in the Sky © Marjorie Dobson
Christian Organic Husbandry © Ancilla Dent OSB and Geoffrey Duncan
Creator and Sustainer of the Earth © Kevin Fray
Dance of Creation, The © David Pickering
Dearest Earth, Our Mother © William L Wallace
Gum Trees, The © Bernard Thorogood
Healing Power of Bamboo, The © Anil Kumar Patil
Healing Power of Red Gum Tree, The © Anil Kumar Patil
Hungry Ones, The © Words and Music, Cecily Taylor. Music is published in
                                        New Orbit, Stainer and Bell Ltd.,

Leaping into Spring © David J Harding
Litany for Eco-justice, A © Diann Neu
Litany of Hope, A © Neil Thorogood
Living Water © Kevin Fray
Living Waterways © Dave Bookless
LOAF Principles, The © Barbara Echlin
Longdendale Psalm © Janet Lees

Meeting, The © Pat Randall
New Heaven and A New Earth, A © R J McKelvey
Our Relationship with the Earth © William L Wallace
Out of the Ark © David Mowbray
Prayer of Intercession, A © Neil Thorogood
Prayer of Praise and Thanksgiving, A © Neil Thorogood
Promising © David J Harding
Rubber Tree, The © Anil Kumar Patil
Song of God's Goodness, A © William Whitson
Thus Comes Love © Cecily Taylor
Tree of Life © Peter Graystone
Twittering, Leaping, Soaring, Playing © David Pickering
Voice of Nature, The © David J Harding
What Better Way? © David J Harding

Global Perspectives

All You Powerful Things, Praise the Lord © Peter Graystone
Beautiful Carved Ball, A © Liz Gentil
Benefit for the Earth, A © Pamela Pavitt
Bring Resurrection © Peter Graystone
Bushmen © Survival International
Callum's Different Holiday © Grace Westerduin and Callum Broadley
Celebrating the Uniqueness of Trees © Pax Christi, The Philippines
Charente, The © Margot Arthurton
Creation in Travail © R J McKelvey
Creation Seen – Creation Unseen © Peter Graystone
Creative Carelessness © Marjorie Dobson
Deep in the Core of the Earth © Heather Phillips
Desert Landscape with Nomads © Grace Westerduin
Drought © Margot Arthurton
Earth Credo © Elizabeth Tapia
Earthspin © Liz Sharma
Ecological Footprints © Martyn Goss
El Nino – Source Unknown
Fragility and Strength © Bernard Thorogood
From Swords into Ploughshares © Dom Dinis Sengulane, Mozambique
and Christian Aid

Healing Creation © David Pickering
I Dreamed of A Perfect World © Barbara Oakes, Ashton-in-Makerfield
Ikebana © Geoffrey Duncan
In the beginning ... © David Pickering
It Is Not Fair © David J Harding
Land is Holy, The © John Johansen-Berg
Lord of the Wind © Toni Allfrey
May the Blessing of the Earth © Jean Mortimer
Monotheistic Reflection on Pagan Cycles of the Year, A, Andrew Pratt
© Stainer and Bell Ltd

Multi-Coloured Glory © Stephen Brown
Needed – Creative Thinking © Dakshine Chitra
Paradise of Monsters, A © Dick Avi
Positive Husband, A © Geoffrey Duncan/BasicNeeds U K/India
Prayer for Sensitive Travellers, A © Kevin Fray
Prayer from A Psychiatric Environment, A © Roger Grainger
Prayers from Cumbria © Marlene Phillips
Prayer of Repentance, A © Neil Thorogood
Precaution © Cecily Taylor
Rainforest, The © John Seed
Rainsong © Margot Arthurton
Rosy Periwinkle, Source Unknown
Tide Turning © David Pickering
Towards Pleasant Lands © Geoffrey Duncan
Tread Gently © Jenny Spouge
What a World © Bernard Thorogood
Wisdom of the Chipmunk, The © Eleanore Milardo
With Her Rucksack on Her Back © Ruth Duncan

To Earn Our Rice and Bread

Basmati Takeaway © Action Aid
Combine Harvester © John Johansen-Berg
Daily Rice or Maize Instead © Basil Bridge
Donkey Plough, A ? © Intermediate Technology Development Group
Fair Trade in Mauritius © Traidcraft
For A Few Pence More © The Fairtrade Foundation
From A Paper Maker © Loreta Capistrano
Fruits of Earth, an extract from the hymn This is Our Prayer © Cecily Taylor
Give With Love © Colin Ferguson
God of the Workplace © Kevin Fray
Heading for the Beach © Fiona Ritchie Walker
Heart of Heaven – Heart of Earth © Agenda Cultural Comunica 1999
Honduras/Judith Escribano, Christian Aid
Little Shark, The © Christopher Gillham
Meditation on a Mange-tout Pea © Janet Lees
Paper from Mulberry Bark © Grace Westerduin
Prayer Reflection, A © Neil Thorogood
Self Worth © Sourubarani, Sri Lanka
Shakuhachi (Bamboo Flute) © Anil Kumar Patil
Sower and Reaper Rejoice Together © Linda Jones /CAFOD
Thoughts over a Grapefruit Juice and a Sesame Bun © Geoffrey Duncan
To Attain Their Noble Dreams © Salay/Traidcraft
We Have a Job Because of You © Traidcraft

Greening the Congregation

All the items in this section are copyright of Eco-Congregations
Challenge for a Green Life Style

Eco-Congregation
Green Sermons and Green Decisions
Grounding in Faith
Growing in Faith
Let's Get Real
Living in Faith
Managing in Faith
Premises Reflect Mission Priorities
Through Word and Deed
Wildflowers for God
Wonder of God's Creation

Make Justice Flow

Arms Trade and the Environment © David Binns
Cry for Our Poor, The © Pat Randall
Daily Offerings © Wendy D Ward
Gleanings © Geoffrey Duncan and Pamela Pavitt
African Willow, The
Car Parking Charges
Cost of Travel, The
Dodo, The
Island Treasures
Lemon Snow
Our Recycling Bins
Scuttling Around the Namibian Desert
Water Needed for Life
Global Market © Linda Jones/CAFOD
God of Creation © Martyn Goss
Great Trees © Barnard Thorogood
Help Counter Global Warming © Council for World Mission
Lament of a Consumerist © Erna Colebrook
Last House, The © Cecily Taylor
Litany for Forgiveness, A © Kate Compston
Loving God Creator of Earth and Heaven © Martyn Goss
Maori Perspective, A © Leigh Bredenkamp
One Single World © David J Harding
Pacific Context, A © Leigh Bredenkamp
Prayers for Fair Values © The Fairtrade Foundation
Profound Moments © Janet Wootton
Seeds of the Kingdom © Linda Jones/CAFOD
Share My Lunch © Geoffrey Duncan/Association of People with Disability
Share the Harvest © Linda Jones/CAFOD
Story for Our Time, A © Martyn Goss
Tip the Balance © Sophie Stanes
Twenty Years On © Geoffrey Duncan
Work for the Peace of the City © David G Cornick

All items of Textile Art © Pamela Pavitt

Photographs on pages 41, 97, 146, 171 © Geoffrey Duncan

Photographs on pages 107, 157, 159, 163, 183 © Pamela Pavitt

Photographs - 'Do not harm the earth' page 61
and 'Look at the birds of the air' page 81 ©   Soichi Watanabe
Soichi Watanabe lives and paints in Japan where he is a member of the
United Church of Christ in Japan. Between 1986 and 2002, he has held
eight solo exhibitions. Many of his illustrations are in religious
publications, including one by the Japan Bible Society.

The Image of 'the bird that wants to survive' by Fiel Dos Santos was
photographed by Paul Hackett © Christian Aid. Used with permission.

The Donkey Plough? - line drawings - © Intermediate Technology
Development Group

The Maze © Pamela Pavitt (inserted sheet)

The samples of paper used in the background on pages 142-143
are available from Traidcraft.

The title page backgrounds are images of recycled paper made with
shredded bank notes.